Salvation LIFE BOOKS

Spiritual Formation

Wesleyan Perspective

SalvationLife.com

**HOW GOD SHAKES, RATTLES AND ROLLS
OUR EASY-LISTENING LIVES**

ROBERT C. PELFREY

SalvationLife Books
www.salvationlife.com/books
E-mail: daniel@salvationlife.com

Copyright © 2014 Robert C. Pelfrey

All rights reserved. No part of this book may be reproduced in any form without written permission from SalvationLife Books.

ISBN-10: 0692022635
ISBN-13: 978-0692022634

Cover design: Roy Migabon: roymigabon.weebly.com

Unless otherwise noted, scripture quotations are from THE HOLY BIBLE, NEW INTERNATIONAL VERSION®, NIV® Copyright © 1973, 1978, 1984, 2011 by Biblica, Inc.® Used by permission. All rights reserved worldwide.

For Jamie
Rocking my world since 1999
You wreck me, baby...

I will proclaim the name of the Lord.
Oh, praise the greatness of our God!
He is the Rock...
-Moses in Deuteronomy 32:3-4

...on this Rock I will build my church...
-Jesus in Matthew 16:18

For those about to Rock, we salute you!
-AC/DC in 1981

CONTENTS

Acknowledgements	9
Introduction	11

REBELLION

1. Rebel Yell	14
2. Rebel God	19
3. Beggar's Banquet	26
4. Jesus is a Lousy Dinner Guest	29

RIFFS

5. Riff God	34
6. The Faith Riff: Crossing the Bridge	41
7. The Justice Riff: A Person's a Person	56
8. The Peace Riff: Us and Them	67
9. The Care Riff: The God of Dirty Hands	75
10. The Beauty Riff: Anecdote of Three Jars	85

Rhythm

11. Rhythm God	94
12. Beat 1: God Coming	101
13. Beat 2: God Dying	108
14. Beat 3: God Rising	128
15. Beat 4: God Making All Things New	138

Road

16. Road God	148
17. Wanderers	153
18. The Cycle of Becoming	158
19. The New World	162

Roots

20. Rock God	166
21. Redemption	172

Notes	179
About the Author	183

ACKNOWLEDGEMENTS

Guy Dees saw something in me and invited me to work with him in youth ministry among the amazing kids of Coulter Road Baptist church in Amarillo, Texas, and Valley Baptist Church in Bakersfield, California. Guy was the first person to put me in a real leadership role, especially in a church setting, and my life has never been the same as a result of his belief, his mentoring, and his friendship.

I got to live out my rock and roll dreams, first in the 80s, with my high school and college bandmates: Andy Lemons, Don Sheffield, Mike Sheffield, Roger McGallian, and Kiley Breitling, plus honorary bandmate and lifelong brother, Thomas McKenzie. Then, in the 90s, in my band Crossroads: Roger, Kiley, Shani Steinbeck Smith, Darsen Sowers, and the late, great David Busa, plus honorary bandmate and lifelong brother, Chad Mantooth. It was only a providential gift of God that I was blessed to come of age among such outstanding talent and loving friends.

The ideas and faith reflected in this book have been forged in pastoral ministry with the people of St. Luke United Methodist Church in Lexington, Kentucky; St. Paul's United Methodist Church in Amarillo, Texas; Elmwood West United Methodist Church in Abilene, Texas; and First United Methodist Church of Midland, Texas. These dear saints are the kind of loving people you read about in the Bible and in church history, and I've been blessed to live and work among them.

My partner in writing, publishing, conversation, and all things spiritual formation is Daniel Harris. He has been there for me and taught me in more ways than he knows. I am thankful for his friendship, his heart, his gifts, and his brotherhood.

My brother, John, taught me to play guitar and laid the foundation for pretty much everything I would come to learn and love about rock and roll. My parents, Betty and Michael, taught me the Christian faith but, much more, have modeled the unconditional love of Christ consistently throughout my life. A son could not ask for a better gift. I am blessed with an astoundingly loving and supportive family, including Sandra and David, and words fail to express my deep and eternal gratitude.

My life forever changed in the best possible way when Madison Jane Pelfrey was born. She is my precious daughter and my sister in Christ who has made me aware of love so unspeakably powerful that it lives as a constant ache in my soul. I've written this book to help her "seek first God's kingdom and his righteousness" (Matt. 6:33)...and to help her rock!

And then there's Jamie. Every great love song and power ballad was written about her. She has shown me the abiding love of God, the kind of love you move in to and make your home. I would cross oceans and deserts, climb mountains and push through crowded masses, just to be with her. But the great blessing of my life is, she's right by my side.

S.D.G.

INTRODUCTION

STAND UP AND BE COUNTED for what you are about to receive.[1]

This, brothers and sisters, is rock and roll. It is in our cars and in our schools, at work and in our bedrooms, on TV and in the streets. It is in our hearts, in our souls, in our minds, and in our strength. It is a force to be reckoned with. It is here to stay. It will never die.

We're still talking about rock and roll, right? Maybe. Maybe not. I'm about to pull a fast one. I'm going to talk about rock and roll and God at the same time, sometimes in the same sentence (like this one). I'm going to deal with concepts like life in union with God and his kingdom through mindfulness, knowledge, and will. And I'm going to deal with the genius of people like Buddy Holly and Bruce Springsteen.

I'm going to talk about rock and roll's Rebellion. But what I'm really talking about is awakening, about intentionally turning from blindly marching toward the death of worldly conformity to formation in the eternal image of Jesus Christ the Son of God.

I'm going to talk about rock and roll's Riffs. But what I'm really talking about is how we can learn to deeply know God's nature and character and to recognize God's activity in our lives and in the world in which we live, and then to join him.

I'm going to talk about rock and roll's Rhythm. But what I'm really talking about is learning to walk with God, to share life with God through daily and weekly patterns, through the natural seasons and progression of life, and through annually sharing in God's story.

I'm going to talk about rock and roll on the Road. But what I'm really talking about is how God is at work right alongside us, in every place and every life, transforming the everyday world around us into nothing less than the kingdom of God, and calling us to follow him.

I'm going to talk about rock and roll's Roots. But what I'm really talking about is how God is with us, and about the tension that results from his work of redemption in us and through us as slavery and liberation confront each other in a collision of kingdoms, all in this world.

I'm not really trying to fool anybody. It's right there in the title. We're going to talk about Rock and we're going to talk about God. I promise you, the twain shall meet. There will be some sharp turns along the way. We'll be talking about Jimi Hendrix and, before you know it, we're talking about Jesus. We'll talk about Bob Dylan and, surprise, we're talking about the church. We'll cover some other things too – movies, sports, art, some personal anecdotes – but I'll be pretty clear pretty quickly, breaking things down as reasonably as I can. I'm not trying to hide anything. I just want us to spend a little time together, and maybe I can share some things that I've picked up through years of studying and following and listening and worshiping and trying to love…and from a lifetime of rocking. I pray our time together will be meaningful, enlightening, encouraging, and even a little fun.

But I'll warn you: it might get loud.

PART I
REBELLION

Tomorrow belongs to those who can hear it coming.
- David Bowie

ONE

REBEL YELL

IT STARTS WITH A YELL. Crying from the depths of oppression. Celebrating the joy of liberation. Wailing in the dark night of the soul. Writhing in the throes of passion. Inciting revolution. Indicting institutions. Inviting absolution. Whatever the situation, there's a yell. It's Jesus yelling about the religious hypocrites and his own forsakenness, calling for the thirsty sinners to come and for the thieves in the Temple to go. It's The Who's Roger Daltrey yelling that it's a teenage wasteland and we won't get fooled again, or James Brown yelling that he feels good. It's the psalmist longing to take the enemy's infants and dash them against the rocks, and Metallica's James Hetfield yelling about being imprisoned by darkness and absolute horror. It's the lover of Song of Songs yelling for his love to come away with him, and Bruce Springsteen yelling, "Baby, we were born to run!" It's King David and Bono and all of humanity yelling, "How long?! How long…" Often there are no words – just a sound from the deepest waters of the soul's well. It's an expression of what it is to be a reasonable, self-controlled human being experiencing more life than can be understood or dismissed. Is it coming from the Scriptures or from my speakers? "Glory!" "Hey!" "Hallelujah!" "Help!" "Rock!" "Roll!" "Save my soul!" "Wop-bop-a-loo-bop, a-lop bam boom!" It's a yell and it's rock and roll.

* * *

"Christianity is not the way. *Christ* is the way." Preachers have those moments that cause trouble...if they're doing it right, anyway. That was one of mine, that line about Christianity not being the way. It ruffled feathers. So much so that I had a couple folks walk out and one even left the church. It may seem clear to you what I meant....it did to me. Jesus did not come to start a new religion, and it is not the empty observance of religious tenets that brings us into relationship with God. I was just quoting the guy – Jesus – letting him speak for himself. "I am the way to the Father," he said. But whenever you let Jesus speak for himself, look out!

Preachers have a way of smoothing over his words, making excuses for him. "This is what he *really* meant," we say. I didn't do that in that sermon and it angered people. As long as we have God safely packed into platitudes and practices, we're all good. The fact that God likely isn't even there doesn't faze us. We'd be bothered if he were there, really. Don't get me wrong. Christianity is fine – wonderful even – to the extent that it points to Christ. I'm not even one of those "it's not a religion, it's a relationship" people, true as that may be. A tradition that exists for regularly and intentionally – religiously – practicing prayer and study and fellowship and worship and service, ordered within the life of the Father, Son, and Holy Spirit, seems good to me. But when we use our well-rehearsed religiosity to force God out, it dies and takes us along with it.

Meanwhile, God is outside but alive and wild. And sometimes God yells. God doesn't yell like we yell. God doesn't even yell like we think God yells. God's yell is louder than tornadoes and earthquakes and wildfires, yet somehow it is the sound of deep silence (1 Kgs. 19:11-13).

We're scared of the yell. We don't know what to do with it. Can we ever get to the point that our yell is also the sound of that deep silence? Is there a purpose for the yell, or is it just shouting into the violent wind? Because the tragedy of it all is that the yell is life, or I should say the yell is our aliveness. It's inside us, but we've muffled it under appearances and consumption and fear and comfort. We are a genteel people. We are domesticated and safe – buttoned down and buttoned up – seeking to keep things in our control and watering them down in the process. While it isn't good to paint with too broad a brush, it would be reasonably accurate to say that an upwardly-mobile 21st century American Christian, who defines faith largely as an occasional hour spectating in anonymous mega-worship, a "Christian" radio station among the car radio presets, and a voting record carefully adhering to the misguidance of media pundits who have the kingdom of ratings at heart, is a far cry from the rabble-rousing early Christians who got arrested and killed rather than shrink into polite pagan society and the cult of emperor-worship.

What if God is just as present – or even more so – in the streets outside that church, in the songs on another radio station, in the politics of the other party…or none at all? What if God wants to crank it up, rail against our institutions, and dance with us in the slums? What if God is the yell? What if God is a Rock God? What would that make us?

The leather-belted, hair-shirted wild man, John the Baptist; the shaven-headed imprisoned trouble-maker, Paul; the passionate rebellious youth, Timothy; foul-mouthed blue collar fishermen; former prostitutes, drunks, and cheats; mothers and widows and wealthy business-ladies and serial brides and all manner of women who don't keep to their place; families who let prophets and preachers and a homeless messiah crash on their couch for a while; the Son of God who takes away sin by loving sinners and who heralds God's kingdom by turning boring water into wine…*good* wine – this is who we are. And who we are is rock and roll.

Obviously it isn't the clothes or hairstyles or any cultural categories that make us rock and roll. If it were then we would just be posers, and posers are *not* rock and roll. It's really not even the music – there are hymns and country songs and jazz and classical pieces that are more rock and roll than many rock songs. It's the attitude behind these things that makes them, and us, rock and roll. More than anything it's the Rock God in whose image we're made that makes us rock and roll. There's an in-your-face rebellion, a raucous hands-in-the air approach to life that just can't abide blindly marching toward a cliff of worldly status quo. There's a yell inside you. It may be loud or quiet, confrontational or reserved, angry or joyful. But it is grounded in the profound sound of sheer silence. And it crackles with the same electricity that had Jesus turning over tables and Jimi Hendrix burning and smashing his guitar.

Stay with me. I know Jesus and Jimi did not exactly have the same agenda. But we might be surprised where the Rock God turns up. It is Jimi's story (and can be seen on the original lyric sheet) that "Purple Haze" was originally titled "Purple Haze – Jesus Saves," and was inspired by a nightmare out of which Jimi claims he was saved by his faith in Jesus. And Jesus and Jimi were about love, though their understanding of love had some marked differences. But where Jesus and Jimi really line up is in upsetting the establishment.

In the act of setting his guitar on fire and smashing it to pieces at the Monterey Pop Festival in 1967, Jimi Hendrix was taking the primary instrument of rock and roll and utterly dismantling it, thereby challenging all it stood for. "You think rock and roll is this guitar, this music?" he was saying. "No! *This* is rock and roll!" Smash! (Fitting that he did this while playing the song "Wild Thing.") He even introduced the performance by saying, "I'm gonna sacrifice something that I really love."

So Jesus strolls into the Jewish Temple, the faintly beating, adulterous heart of first-century Jewish life and identity, and he fulfills ancient prophecy – God returning to his Temple, tellingly unrecognized. He sees the corruption and fruitlessness of his people and he turns the place on its head by turning over the tables of the thieves who were selling sacrificial animals at criminally inflated prices. "You think being God's people is this empty ritual, this hypocrisy?" he was saying. "No! *This* is what it means to be God's people!" Smash! He utterly dismantles the primary "instrument" of sacrificial worship. Then he becomes the sacrifice. That's rock and roll.

TWO

REBEL GOD

A ROCK AND ROLL GRAMMAR LESSON: As a noun, rock and roll is a kind of music. You know this. You've heard it. You probably like it, at least some of it. A story in Buddhism instructs that the words of the sacred writings point to enlightenment like a finger points to the moon. Once the moon has been found, the finger is no longer necessary. The reason for using rock and roll as a "finger" to point to God is that it points us to aspects of God that we don't often see, typically because we're scared to look. And, while it might be said that rock and roll has traditionally been about "giving the finger" of a different kind, in its guts it is ideally suited to point us in the right direction. If this offends, then it is proving the point. We could do with a little offense. As I once heard Motörhead's Lemmy Kilmister posit, "Who do they think they are that they shouldn't be offended?"[2] While I'm certainly not encouraging obscene gestures or offending for the sake of offending, I am suggesting that we might need a little of the offense that rock and roll has to offer. We definitely need the offense that God has to offer.

And speaking of offense, there's rock and roll the verb. It is commonly understood that this particular musical hybrid of rhythm and blues, country and western, and gospel took its name from a description of the sex act – rocking and rolling. If there wasn't a disconnect at "the finger," then there is typically a disconnect at this point. We heirs of puritan values don't speak of such things (despite the fact that the Puritans prided themselves on having large numbers of children...you do the math), and an art form that celebrates such worldliness has no place in polite Christian conversation.

I would not insult your intelligence by pretending that the verb rock and roll has much to do with monogamous Christian marriage (though it needn't be otherwise). But I also would not insult your intelligence by perpetuating the stereotype that there is no place for such talk among Christians. Why shouldn't Christians celebrate sex as part of God's intention for his creation? Indeed, what might happen if Christian married couples weren't so long-faced and prudish about rocking and rolling? You may be blushing right now, again proving the point. The Old Testament book *Song of Songs* (that great name basically means "the songiest of all songs") is an entire biblical book that uses the language of romantic and erotic love to celebrate passion and to point to the ideal intimate relationship between God and humanity. So you can see that even the original, verbal meaning of rock and roll is not so far from biblical imagery used to point us to God. However, with this original connotation largely a dusty piece of etymological history, today "rock and roll" as a verb carries a more general sense of letting oneself be caught up by the spirit of life – connected to that rebel yell – as in the celebratory cry, "Let's rock and roll!"

It seems the verb came first, then the noun, and more recently we've begun using "rock and roll" as an adjective. This usage is at once the most superficial and the deepest. On the superficial level, it is describing appearance and fashion choices. With changing times it was not unusual for blue jeans or bell-bottoms or spandex, a pompadour or a mop-top or bleached spikes, a motorcycle or a GTO, tattoos, piercings, or any number of edgy elements to be described as "rock and roll," as in, "That's so rock and roll!" But considered more deeply, what is being said is that these superficial elements are reflecting the deeper rebellious spirit of rock and roll. Another example might be, "A rock and roll grammar lesson is *not* very rock and roll." You get the idea.

* * *

A rock and roll riddle:

Is a punk band still a punk band after it signs a record contract?

Giving over artistic control to a big record company is not in keeping with punk's anarchistic ethos – not very "punk" (another fun adjective stemming from "rock and roll"). The band maintains its key downwardly-mobile elements of a junkies-who-just-woke-up appearance, cacophonous no-rules music, and an overall public belligerence. But now they're getting paid to maintain these elements. The things that made them authentically punk – they really were junkies who slept in their clothes; they didn't know or care how to sing or write a proper song; their belligerence stemmed from being societal outcasts – those things are now part of a slickly marketed product. And now they are at the mercy of a corporate kiss-up who leases a Beemer and sits in a corner office in a 21st century Tower of Babel, dreaming of more.

And with that, I present the church in 21st century America:

The church used to be rebellious and raw and underground. The church used to be very rock and roll, even punk. Not so much anymore. Oh, there are certainly elements of the true spirit, wherever there's the true Spirit. The yell is still in there. But all too often the church in America today is caught up in one cult of personality after another. It allows itself to be the pawn of political parties. It plays the harlot after wealth and empire, power and fame. The church in America today is often a bloated has-been prancing about in a sequined jumpsuit and cape, so caught up in marketing and sales and indulging its worldly appetites that it has lost the fire and hunger that once fueled its original guitar-smashing, thunderous passion. You don't like what I'm saying? Then listen to the yell. It's time to rebel.

God is a rebel God. He's not a rebel god like Iggy Pop and Lou Reed, but a big-"G" God who reveals himself in rebellion against the constraints and puffed chests of would-be worldly authorities. Now to be clear, God is not really rebelling as some identity-seeking teenager trying to anger his parents, because God is not subject to whims of ego and life phases driven by insecurity. As with the other aspects of rock and roll presented here, as well as most divinely-attributed anthropomorphisms presented in Scripture and history, this is merely an attempt to grasp the ungraspable. Of all the attributes of rock and roll that characterize it and God, rebellion stands front and center (well, probably off-center). And, rebellion being what it is, it is the very inability to define both rock and roll and God that makes rebellion so fitting. Ironically, this is the aspect of rock and roll that makes it so anathema to many Christians. It is also the aspect of God that keeps us from really letting go and following him, and that has me insisting on my god-in-a-box over yours, and vice versa.

It's nothing to say Jesus was a rebel. Even total squares began thinking they were cool – "relevant" was the buzzword – by saying such things in the 1980s. They were trying desperately to show the culture how cool Jesus is, with T-shirts and bumper stickers and church production value and worship music that was a nice brand of rock and roll lite. But what they were doing was corporatizing Jesus, casting his image as something sellable. What they were doing was taking the Lord's name in vain. (Anyone can use "God" or "Jesus" as a curse word. It takes deep depravity to use him to build a self-aggrandizing empire.) So, in the very act of dragging Jesus into a faux-rebellion, they were really just cleaning him up and getting him camera-ready. Not very rock and roll at all.

* * *

The thing is – now lean in close for this one – we don't have a freaking clue what we're dealing with. This is the God who brought forth a watery chaos, took it in hand, and fashioned a cosmos. Look at some of the ways God reveals himself prior to the Incarnation – among wind, cloud, and fire. This is a God that cannot be gotten hold of. And throughout accounts of his dealings with humanity, his is a voice that is inciting riots and rebellion: declaring creation's curse, flooding the earth, confusing languages and scattering nations, calling Abraham away from his homeland to somewhere unknown and eventually sending him up a mountain to sacrifice his miraculous son, sending Moses into the thick of hostility to lead the people through a sea and into an exilic wasteland, and then on and on through priests and judges and kings and prophets. Who do we think we are, trying to tame him? This rebel God is crazy!

But most amazing of all, he again takes these seemingly chaotic elements in hand and fashions his own glorifying ends. We can't do that. All of our empires and governments and laws, our harnessing the forces of nature and articulating the mysteries of science, our capacities for beauty and horror and organization and destruction, nothing we can do or be can approach either the chaos or the order of God. This doesn't stop us from trying, which is mostly good because it's the trying that brings out the best in us – art, innovation, breakthroughs. But it's also the trying that brings out our worst, exposing our seemingly limitless capacity to make war and to exalt ourselves and to step on the throat of the earth until it has coughed out its last breath. And on God goes, throwing an elbow in our general direction and marching forward with his plans for creating a universe. That's rebellion.

And need we even go into the Christ event? Jesus is the true physical embodiment of divine rebellion. Look at him trampling waves underfoot, marching across the watery chaos as if on dry ground. Watch him heal diseases and raise the dead as if even the laws of life and death have no bearing in his presence. See him turn bland water into fine wine and miraculously multiply bread and fish to feed the masses, shedding new light on disciplines as disparate as chemistry and supply-and-demand, not to mention sending up a huge sign that the old order is done and he is the new. And at every turn, hear him confound and rebuke the would-be authorities that trip over their tongues to put God in his place. In Jesus we see God repurposing the laws of nature, of science, of government and economics, of social sciences and justice and power, and even the religious laws his own people would claim were handed down by God himself. What he is really doing is ushering in a new kingdom with its own overarching law of love, exposing the ineptitude of our attempts and the bankruptcy of our posturing.

It all culminates in perhaps his greatest act of rebellion: the cross. We typically focus, and rightly so, on the cross as Jesus' ultimate act of obedience. But in the face of the world's systems of power and twisted misunderstandings about empire and immortality, the cross is the ultimate act of rebellion. Behold the man, the rebel King of heaven and earth: a crucifixion for his coronation; thorn branches for his crown; nails for his scepter and footstool; and a cross for his throne, upon which he hangs to survey his cursing, cowering subjects. He is brutally and publicly shamed, a first-century lynching to show passersby that this naked, bloody mess is what happens when you rebel against the world's authorities. No one would look upon this chaotic scene and see the greatest triumph in the history of the world...no one except God. For in that rebellious act God grabs the chaos of human sin and the death of all creation, takes it in his bloody hands, and fashions redemption. Using death to kill death, he rebels against the grave and rises to inaugurate the new creation. You think God isn't rebellious? That's rebellion.

We'll do our best to understand it, to give it doctrinal labels and argue about who has it all figured out. But we'll never have a clue. It's time to fall into that rebellion and let it knock us around. We mustn't don Christian t-shirts and bumper stickers and post snide comments on social media and call it rebellion; or, worse, turn our church sanctuaries into high-tech lemonade stands and pander for customers. Jesus said anyone who wants to follow him must deny themselves and take up their cross. So it's time to shed the sequined jumpsuits. It's time to destroy our idols and free our minds from cults of personality. It's time to get in the faces of our lawmakers instead of at their other end, and to herald the coming of a different kingdom. It's time to deny ourselves, take up our crosses, and follow Jesus. Follow him all the way – to scorn, to sacrifice, to rejection, to death, and on through to the life that really is life. We'll take all the sin and fear and power-hunger and world-conformity and me, me, me! and all the chaos we're drowning in and let it all die. We'll rebel against the American dream and what Washington and Hollywood and Wall Street and Madison Avenue tell us our lives should be. And we'll set out for that undiscovered country whose music already beckons and whose King is the Rock God.

THREE

BEGGAR'S BANQUET

HERE'S A TOUGH ONE: A king is throwing a wedding banquet for his son. After the mucky-mucks and all the right people refuse to come, the king orders that *everyone* – even the riff-raff – should be invited. We like that part. But then when the king shows up, he finds this one guy not wearing a tuxedo and he tosses the guy out. We don't talk about that part.

Jesus has a way of getting on my nerves sometimes, as he does with this parable (Matt. 22:1-14). He gets on my nerves when he catches me off guard and when I don't understand him. He's *supposed* to stop at that part where everyone gets to come. The chosen ones are too good and/or too busy, so the servants go out to the streets and the slums and make everyone feel cherished and special by inviting them to this sumptuous banquet.

The camera shifts to the banquet hall, to the grand double-doors where homeless vets are dropping their "will work for food" signs and filling their plates at the banquet table; where prostitutes are tugging awkwardly at their short skirts and sitting down in the company of the king; where even corrupt Wall Street golden boys are coming empty-handed to stand at the back of a line that stretches out the door. The camera pans back to reveal the line of invited undesirables stretching across the grounds, out the front gate, and down the street. The music comes up as the credits roll. The End?

No, because at least one guy doesn't have the right clothes? So he's outta there!

Cut! What are you doing, Jesus?! You messed up the whole story!

I think the irritation comes from the subtlety and seeming randomness, characteristic of a parable. There's a scene that I think is understood for Jesus, but which the movie needs to show to make sense of it all. After getting their fill at the banquet, the homeless vet gets up and finds an old dealer friend and the two go off into a room and start shooting heroin; the prostitute starts hitting on the groomsmen to try and drum up some business; the Wall Streeters make crooked business deals with unsuspecting guests at the dinner table. Everyone has a good time while widows sit alone at their kitchen tables and orphans forage for food in the dumpsters. Everyone howls that they have a new place to party while the king and his son are utterly ignored. But we're at the banquet, so everything is fine, right?

It may not be heroin or prostitution or white-collar crime, but overeating or pornography or consumerism will do nicely. We each have our stinky rags that we parade around in as if we're fine. Well, for most of us the stinky rags are our underwear. Outwardly we dress ourselves up. We keep our rot to ourselves, satisfied that we're at the banquet. We're satisfied that we're telling everyone they're ok: "God loves you and your cute little cancerous corruption..." Oh, we might pick and choose a few things we don't like, a few *types* we don't allow: "You can't stay at the banquet and be ____!" But usually we let ourselves, our type, off the hook.

It's not enough to come to the banquet. We also have to change our clothes. We don't change to get in – we're invited guests, after all. But keeping company with the king must change us. Coming to the feast means we've left darkness and slavery and death outside. We can return to it if we want. We can stand outside in the dark and gnash our teeth if we choose. And we do go out to bring the light and the invitation to others. But we don't get to be children of the dark anymore if we also want to live in the light. We don't get to play dress-up in beggar's rags.

The king seems to have something to say about it. Of course he loves you, even in your filth – that's why you're invited. But the beauty and majesty of the king makes us come undone, makes us realize that we are unclean people from an unclean culture and an unclean world (Is. 6:1-8). Why do we get so upset that the king would offer us radiant robes in exchange for our filthy rags? Because, yes, if we come to the wedding, then the king has something to say to us. We come as we are, but we just can't stay that way. And would we really want to? If we think we would, then a glimpse of the king and his kingdom will rid us of any thoughts about clinging to the old self (Eph. 4:17-24). No, the king has some expectations for us, purposes and plans for us. But change hurts. Some of the things he has to say might get on your nerves. It might make you uncomfortable. But the king just doesn't seem too concerned about that. He's infinitely and intimately interested in you...every bit of you. You're invited to the feast, but your host has some new clothes for you. They're uniquely you, but still something new. You sure you want to come to this party?

FOUR

JESUS IS A LOUSY DINNER GUEST

JESUS IS A LOUSY DINNER GUEST. You think it'd be fun to sit at the table and talk to Jesus. "Turn my Diet Coke into wine, Jesus. What is *your* position on the Middle East? We're running low on bread and fish. Could you, you know…?" But Jesus isn't always one for pleasantries, especially in a house where humility and righteousness are lacking. At that point he becomes downright rude.

Jesus? Rude? Oh, often and with gusto! Rebellious might be a better term than rude, especially when he's rebelling against unjust social conventions. There's the story about Jesus going to dinner – on the Sabbath, no less – at the home of a prominent Pharisee (Luke 14:1-24). Now, in Jesus' defense, everyone is staring at him, waiting for him to slip up. But staring is all they do. It's funny to picture, really – all these uppity dinner guests with their eyes agog and mouths hanging open. First, there's a sick man there and Jesus asks everyone at the table if it's ok for him to heal this guy on the Sabbath. They don't say anything. They just stare at him. So he heals the poor guy and sends him on his way. Then Jesus, knowing that they're inwardly judging him for doing "work" on the Sabbath, presses them and asks if they should rescue one of their oxen if it fell into a ditch on the Sabbath. Or how about one of their children? Nothing. Silence. Staring.

Perhaps sensing he hasn't offended everyone enough, Jesus just outright insults all of them. Earlier he had noticed the dinner guests vying for the best seats at the table. So he decides to comment on that, telling a not-so-subtle parable about some wiser guests at, oh I don't know, let's say a random dinner party, who took the lesser seats and counted on the host to notice and invite them into the better places. How embarrassing to act like you're all that and then be treated otherwise. The exalted will be humbled and the humbled will be exalted.

Now that everyone's feeling good and uncomfortable, Jesus turns to his host. He tells his host, the one who invited him to dinner, that he invited all the wrong people by inviting all the "right" people. He should invite the poor and lame to dinner, those who could never pay him back. Thus he would learn of kingdom, rather than social, repayment. Needless to say, Miss Manners Jesus is not.

All of this, however, illustrates Jesus' lifestyle choice of rebellion, of serving others and not caring what the pretty and powerful people think. This is Jesus' thing, acting out prophecies and lessons, his whole life being an act of prophetic worship, a protest song. Jesus' M.O. is one of the most surprisingly radical concepts in the history of thought and action: grace. Grace has teeth. Grace is rebellion. Grace, like Jesus, seeks not to be served but to serve (Mark 10:45). But it often does so by turning over tables and insulting snooty hypocrites.

If we're not careful, we'll find ourselves growling through gritted teeth, "Right on, Jesus! Way to put those rich snobs in their place!" But we are those dinner guests, vying for power and recognition. We are that host, scratching the backs only of those who will scratch ours in return. We are the ones in the parable Jesus goes on to tell, so busily going about our self-importance that we miss the king's banquet. Yet as the church, we should be the ones out in the street inviting all who will – regardless of status and payback potential – to come and feast.

It is vital that we recognize oppression, because the world often calls it success. It is vital that we recognize the oppressed, because the world often calls them nothing. Grace extends honor and value to all people. Grace seeks the balance of recognizing Jesus as: 1) the true King, high and lifted up; and 2) making his place among humanity's low and trodden down.

* * *

I remember standing in the sanctuary of Dexter Avenue Baptist Church in Montgomery, Alabama, the "cradle of the civil rights movement." I looked at the pulpit from which Martin Luther King, Jr., preached the transformational gospel to a people who were systematically dehumanized solely because of their skin color and ethnic roots – in the middle of the most progressive and civilized and, simultaneously, the most oppressive and destructive century in human history. I couldn't bring myself to stand at that pulpit, but I stood in the silence of the sanctuary and looked at it, imagining Dr. King thundering out the biblical call for justice.

A block up the street is the Civil Rights Memorial, where water pours over a black granite wall that has carved into it King's famous quotation of the prophet Amos, through whom God commanded, "Let justice roll down like waters, and righteousness like an ever-flowing stream" (5:24). It's why individual acts of grace so often lead to whole movements, because grace sweeps people into its flow. Grace is what God is doing with the world. It's his plan, his vision. It's why he came to us and comes to us and stands with us. It has a cleansing power, washing away the filth of the oppressor and restoring the soul of the oppressed. It is the living water that flows from within those who drink from the fountain of becoming, the emerging children of God.

What if a little woman hadn't refused to sit at the back of the bus? What if children hadn't shown up to school and students hadn't sat at lunch counters where their "kind" weren't allowed? What if a preacher hadn't lived and shared his dream? These people did not step out of history books. They stepped out of humble homes and jobs and everyday lives, and only stepped into history books because of their step-by-step journey toward justice. They could easily have been you and me – arms linked, police dogs snapping at our ankles, shielding our faces from fire hoses. If we will walk the way of grace, these *will* be you and me.

Anyone looking for Jesus will find him on that bus, at that lunch counter, assaulted with dogs and fire-hoses, heralding a dream, being sold into sex slavery, losing his blue-collar job to help a CEO buy another vacation home, being raped because a man thinks he can get rid of his AIDS by having sex with a virgin, growing up without parents, without an education, without a vote, without medicine, never ever being told or shown "I love you." Here's Jesus, one of the least just like he said, in case any of his so-called followers are looking (Matt. 25:31-46). Here's Jesus, extending bloody grace by standing in a mess he could rightly ignore, dismiss, or destroy. Here's Jesus, railing against our notions of power and earning and self-righteousness and success. Here's Jesus. And the fact that he's here is grace. It's rebellion. It's a yell. And it's a call.

PART II
RIFFS

These riffs were built to last a lifetime...
- Keith Richards

FIVE

RIFF GOD

CHUCK BERRY DID IT FIRST...well, Robert Johnson was doing it back in the '30s. Heck, who knows where it started? But you hear it opening most great rock songs. Think about the first seconds of "Johnny B. Goode." Or how about Jimmy Page in songs like "Whole Lotta Love" and "Heartbreaker" and, well, just about any Zeppelin song. AC/DC's Angus Young is a master in songs like "Back in Black" and "You Shook Me All Night Long" – that guy's got a million of 'em. Slash is another one in Guns n' Roses songs like "Welcome to the Jungle" and "Sweet Child o' Mine" – nails it! Nails what? The riff. These guys are all masterful riff guitarists.

Think of the acoustic riff in The Violent Femmes' garage classic "Blister in the Sun." There's Elton John's piano in "Tiny Dancer" and the bass on Queen's "Another One Bites the Dust" and "Under Pressure" (shame on you, Vanilla Ice). And there's the anthemic keyboard riff of Van Halen's "Jump," played by one of the greatest guitarists ever. There are many ways to make a great riff. But in the end, the riff's the thing.

The riff is fundamental in blues, jazz and, of course, rock and roll. It's that opening melodic or chordal bit, the motif that establishes the tone and melodic structure of the whole song and will likely appear a few more times. But perhaps what most characterizes a riff is its association with a whole song. You know if it's going to be "Oh, Pretty Woman" or "Sweet

Home Alabama" or "Layla" by the riff. Think about those songs...there's the riff. (Tellingly, Eric Clapton introduced his popular live unplugged version of "Layla" with the challenge, "Let's see if you can spot this one." The reason it was hard to "spot" was that he had changed the famous riff and, yes, it changed the song significantly.) So it's not just a cool instrumental thing that has lots of significance on its own. It's that that instrumental thing – cool as it may be – has significance mainly because it points to the whole song. The lights go out, the opening riff thunders from the speakers, and the hands go into the air because you know that song...you love that song! That's rock and roll.

God is a Riff God. Not a riff god like Jimi Hendrix and Keith Richards, but a big-"G" God who reveals himself and his kingdom in riffs. God reveals himself in the Bible this way. There's the opening riff of God as Creator of all that is, seen and unseen. After it starts things off in Genesis, we hear it again in all kinds of big moments.

There's the starry-sky covenant with Abraham – the Creator-God who made those stars can make a great nation of childless old Abraham and barren Sarah.

There's God reminding a doubtful, stammering Moses who it was who gave people their mouths and ears – this same Creator-God can speak and create wonders through him to overcome Egypt's oppressive regime.

There's God putting desperate, suffering Job on trial with the question, "Where were you when I laid the earth's foundation? Tell me if you understand" (38:4). This Creator-God can give meaning to a life that sees none.

There's David the psalmist's humble affirmation that the Lord made "mere mortals" and "crowned them with glory and honor" (Ps. 8:5) – rightly placed hope from a man after the Creator-God's own heart.

The Gospel of John tells a new creation story as he writes, "In the beginning was the Word...." This Word was with the

Creator-God and the Word is, in fact, the Creator-God (John 1:1).

The apostle Paul picks up this riff in his glorious creedal statement that all things – seen and unseen – are made by and for Jesus, the Creator-Word, who is making all things new.

And then the whole thing ends (re-begins?) with the new heavens and the new earth. In all these the Creator-God riff resonates. And it is heard in the world today – heaven and earth are full of the glory of God riffs. It's an ancient riff, but it somehow points to a new song.

Of course that's just one riff among many. If you'll listen attentively you'll hear.

There are water riffs like the formless void of pre-creation which was literally a "watery chaos," the river that flowed and forked out of Eden, Noah's global flood, the Red Sea that was the passage from slavery to promised-land freedom, Jonah's fishy death and rebirth, John baptizing in the Jordan, Jesus calming a storm and walking on the Sea of Galilee, and the river of life forever flowing through the New Jerusalem. The whole God-song is introduced and concludes with the water riff.

There are tree riffs like Eden's trees of life and of the knowledge of good and evil, Abraham's oak under which he meets the triune Angel-of-the-LORD, the lovers in Song of Songs meeting under an apple tree, wee Zaccheus climbing a sycamore to glimpse Jesus, Jesus cursing a fruitless fig tree, Jesus' cross, and in the New Jerusalem, the tree of life grows and bears different fruit for every month as its leaves grow for the healing of the nations. The whole God-song is introduced and concludes with the tree riff.

And there are grand, sweeping thematic riffs like exile and homecoming – heard in the Israelites' captivity and exodus and in Jesus' parables like the Prodigal Son and, of course, in the story of humanity's fall and redemption. The whole God-song is introduced and concludes with the exile-and-homecoming riff.

* * *

Picking up on these riffs is really fun. You should try it. You just may find your fist shooting into the air when you hear them. They aren't always readily heard. It often took many generations before Scripture writers could listen back and pick out the riffs. They had to get to a certain point in the God-song before they began to recognize that same riff that had been repeated, and then to work out what God was revealing about himself and relating to creation. Likewise, in our lives, it sometimes takes a while before we begin to pick up on God-riffs, to listen back to the God-song our life is playing and hear the riffs he keeps bringing in. But when we do, when we pick up on them and even learn to play along, we find our lives resounding with nothing less than the music of God. Here's how it works.

Like riffs in rock and roll, God's riffs are little bits that point to the bigger story. And what they are ultimately pointing to are God's kingdom and God himself. Like rock's riffs, these riffs might be interesting by themselves, but they are most interesting and significant to the extent that they point to the whole song, the God-song. So, for example, something like justice is important all by itself. But it takes on a more profound and eternal significance when it reveals something about God, that God is just. And then, when we pick up on the fact that humans are made in God's image – the image riff (Gen. 1:27) – then that justice riff becomes personal as we realize it's part of us and we must play it ourselves. We might work to end local homelessness or global human trafficking, or at least we try to treat others justly. Our lives resonate with God's life as we play his riffs. We become part of his songs. Yes! That's where the fist-pumping starts!

So, riffs like faith and justice and peace and care and beauty – all nice tunes by themselves – become eternal *rock* when we hear them in God, see them as part of our God-imaged selves, and start playing them with our lives. I've had strange dreams every so often while drifting off with music playing. The music is instrumental usually – John Coltrane maybe – and I'll dream that I'm talking to someone, but what's coming out of my mouth is what's coming out of Trane's sax. So I'm talking but it's this glorious, tumbling saxophone music that is coming out. It's your typical weird sort of dream, but it's what I'm getting at here. God is a riff God. And we – made in his image – are riff people, made to be consumed by God-riffs and to be swept up into kingdom songs. God-music should be tumbling out of our lives.

As we begin to learn some fundamental God-riffs like faith, justice, peace, care, and beauty, we also begin to notice their glaring absence. We say to ourselves, "The earth is supposed to be resounding with God's kingdom songs, so why am I not hearing the justice riff...the faith riff...the beauty riff? There should be peace here. These people should be caring for each other. This sounds awful!" Sometimes God's riffs are altogether absent, and sometimes they have been reworked by those who don't really know or care about God's music. This is all the more reason for us to learn the God riffs faithfully, accurately, and to begin to jam with them.

Riffs get so discordant when they are pulled out of the divine songs. They seem okay at first, people trying to play God-riffs apart from the God-song. But eventually they seem more like they have the form of godliness but are missing the power (2 Tim. 3:5), and maybe they don't even have the form. Faith becomes bumper-sticker platitudes and generic spirituality. Justice becomes street-justice, eye-for-an-eye vengeance, "enhanced interrogation techniques." Beauty becomes self-indulgent obsession, superficial lust, a destructive cultural dictatorship. Care of creation becomes pagan nature-worship and care of others becomes dehumanizing institutionalization. And even peace becomes a schmaltzy live-and-let-live homogenization that is apathetic toward truth and the deeper issues that divide people.

But resounding with the Creator, the Redeemer, the sanctifying Sustainer, these riffs become the very music of God's kingdom coming on earth as it is in heaven (I think I heard that one somewhere). The same way you know "Money for Nothing" by Mark Knopfler's buzz-saw fingerpicked guitar riff, so the world begins to know God by listening to the lives of people who have begun to play his songs. And like a kid sitting in his bedroom with the guitar he got for Christmas, banging out elementary riffs like "Iron Man" and "Smoke On the Water," we learn gradually – maybe treating our family and friends justly, making peace with everyday adversaries. The kid moves on to "Wanted Dead or Alive" and "Crazy Train" – we learn the beauty of worship and to care for our elders. And so it goes as the maturing young riffer hits "Voodoo Child" and "Walk This Way" and chord-based riffs that make his hands hurt, like stuff by the Police and U2. Maturing Christians learn to put others before ourselves and to affirm the value of the lowly and to recognize the beauty of things that are only made beautiful in God's grace. Our lives become God-music. We learn the love riff – the riff of all riffs – and it hurts more than our hands. And no one knows this better than the riff God.

* * *

So I'll spend a little time developing some of these basic riffs: faith, justice, peace, care, and beauty. There are many others. You might ask why not the love riff? But love is really the music of each of these riffs being played – at all costs – in our everyday lives. Or how about the holiness riff? Holiness is the total commitment to practice and play all the riffs more authentically and perfectly – more lovingly – the way they are played by God himself.

While these are only a beginning, they are a good beginning. If we can learn to walk by faith, to do justice, to make peace, to care for others, and to live beautifully, we are well on our way to hearing the kingdom music and riffing along with the Rock God.

SIX

THE FAITH RIFF: CROSSING THE BRIDGE

THEN THERE WAS THE TIME Jesus walked into that Starbucks (John 4). The soccer moms had dropped the kids off at school and had been sitting there gossiping. But now they were gone. College students had clicked busily on their laptops. But now only one sat at a corner table, headphones on. Businesspeople had looked at their watches and tapped their feet as they waited in line. But they've gone on to their meetings. Now there was a woman there, clothed and painted to attract the attention of men, and she'd been looking for love in all the wrong places...year after year, husband after husband. Now she's just shacking up with a guy and might be looking for a new one. And Jesus, a young single guy on his own, finds himself in the company of this woman.

She comes during this time of the day to avoid the catty whispers, the reminders of younger days and paths not taken, the strength and goings-on of a community in which she is not welcome. Empty now. There among the woody smell of the coffee and the soothing strains of James Taylor music, Jesus, a miracle worker and up-and-coming rabbi, stands with this woman, a woman of dubious repute and lonely heart. Jesus is in the wrong place at the wrong time with the wrong person... exactly how he seems to like it.

Besides the superficial tension in the scene, there's a deeper divide – one that stretches back dozens of generations. His people despise her people and vice versa, mostly because of empty religion that has given way to a cultural chasm. Her people, the Samaritans, have intermarried with the surrounding gentile nations, and his people, the "pure" Jews, will have nothing to do with them. So the Samaritans are defensive and return the derision. All the more reason for Jesus and this woman to have nothing to do with each other.

He engages her in conversation, connects with her. He calls her on her stuff. She gets defensive. He challenges her misguided notions of personal fulfillment through unhealthy relationships. She dodges the issue and turns to religion. "Hey, who has the monopoly on this God business?" she asks sarcastically. Jesus addresses her religious superiority and affirms that, yes, salvation is coming from the Jews. But he says all this sympathetically.

Shockingly he seems to put them on level ground in the eyes of God. He moves past all this superficial nonsense and gets down to true spirituality. God is not satisfied to drop in and decorate the walls we build for ourselves. God is looking to engage people on the deepest level – in spirit and truth. The Ancient of Days is doing something new, and the new thing is standing right there in Starbucks. The woman is floored. She takes out her phone and calls her friends to come down and meet this guy. Jesus just smiles as the disciples come stumbling through the door, groceries in hand and eyebrows raised.

* * *

"Where is God in all this?" We ask ourselves that question so many times at different points in our lives. Our culture asks that question of the church in the most accusatory way. We don't know what we're supposed to do with the beautiful disaster all around us, not to mention inside us. Just when we think we have it figured out – *this* politician or *that* movie or *this* book or *that* celebrity – it all comes up dry as an old well.

One thing is consistent: Jesus often seems absent from where we expect him, but then he turns up in the most unlikely of places.

And that's just the thing: Jesus is not concerned with keeping up appearances. Jesus is about breaking down the walls that we try so hard to keep up. Rich or poor, black or white, liberal or conservative, church or street – Jesus refuses to obey the rules of polite, middle-class society. Does that scare you? I've watched it scare many people right in the middle of a church worship service. They didn't expect God to actually show up. And the way he showed up – in the testimonies or prayers or tears or joyous worship of "those" kinds of people. The nerve!

And Jesus doesn't just break down our cultural walls, but he invades our hiding places. The teetering little shelters we build for ourselves – co-dependent relationships, substance abuse, celebrity worship, consumption, work, the natural order – Jesus comes along and tears the roof off of these hiding places. Jesus wants us to get over ourselves, to stop sitting in our rooms brooding and to come out and play in the mud. Jesus is undignified. There is something about being undignified that is essential for that most important of God-riffs: faith. Keeping up appearances (we could say "vanity") is in direct opposition to faith because vanity is self-centered, and faith requires us to be God-centered.

Once he gets inside, Jesus gets us in an awkward corner, as he did with the woman at Starbucks. He wouldn't go along with her self-deception, and he won't go along with ours either. He calls us on our stuff. He seems to do this not just once, but often. He looks at the cup of stagnant water we're drinking and offers us fresh water. "But I *know* this water," we say. "This water has been getting me by for a long time." But Jesus doesn't want us just to get by; he wants us to *live*. That's the expression that Jesus uses with this woman at the well: "I will give you *living* water." It's an expression that refers to fresh, flowing water as opposed to stagnant, dirty water. We might say "sparkling" or even "dancing" water. So that's the ultimatum Jesus is putting to us: you can keep living that old, stagnant life or take the plunge into the new, dancing life.

But this is risky. We can feel the warmth of the alcohol or the OxyContin lulling us to oblivion. We can see the pornography on our computer screen or the celebrities on TV and movie screens. We can trick ourselves to believe that one unhealthy relationship after another is real love, or that one more charge on our credit card, one more thing to possess, will give our life some meaning. But Jesus? Where is he? What has he done for me lately?

What Jesus has done for us is kick open the door to the life of faith. The reason Jesus has no use for keeping up appearances is that he is living by faith, not by sight. The reason Jesus finds satisfaction in obeying the unseen Father – he calls this obedience real food and real drink – is because he is living by faith, not by sight. The reason Jesus doesn't care one bit about the things we do to keep ourselves apart from others is because he is all about building a kingdom where everyone listens to and cares for each other, where faith *becomes* sight. The reason Jesus doesn't allow us just to get by with things that give us the *feeling* that we are really living is because he is the one who has opened the eyes of power-blind rulers and the minds of philosophers, warmed the hearts of cold-blooded killers, fed the souls and stomachs of the starving masses, sheltered the beggars and street-fighters, and blanketed the exposed and exploited.

And he comes to each of us in our designer clothes and plasma-screened living rooms and makes us very uncomfortable – just by his being there – because we know that there is something more, and he is it. No more grasping at whatever straws of life we can get hold of. Our lives are seen acts of worship for the unseen God. And that's where it begins and ends: loving God and loving others…completely. Faith means it is no longer about me. Faith means letting go. That is a terrifying thought, but it is the beginning of the authentic faith-life. That's the faith riff. That's the fiery core of the power to become a child of God. When Jesus kicks the door open and the light comes flooding in, it is very startling. But, Oh, the light!

FAITH'S FIRST STEPS

The journey of a thousand miles begins with the first step. These words, attributed to Confucius, are as true of our spiritual pilgrimage through life as they are of a road trip. Faith marks the beginning of the journey and, indeed, faith is really the journey itself. Like Confucius, the writer of the biblical book of Hebrews tells of a first step on a long journey. The journey is that of living life according to an unseen reality, God's reality, and the first step is faith.

This writer defines faith in a couple of different ways (11:1). First, faith is the assurance of things hoped for. With this movement, faith looks forward while changing us now. Faith is so sure of the hoped-for future that it affects the course of our life today. I'm sure that a left on a certain street, a right on the next street, and another right a few blocks down will get me from home to work. I'm sure enough of the journey and destination that I get in the car and pull out of the driveway each morning, and I act on that belief almost every day.

Second, faith is the conviction of things not seen. With this movement, faith looks backward while, again, changing us now. When we clap someone on the back and tell them to "keep the faith," what we mean is to maintain the courageous heart and hope that previously inspired them and others. Likewise, this conviction of things not seen is an overriding belief in the way God has acted in the well-traveled lives of those saints who have gone before, many of whose stories the writer of Hebrews goes on immediately to tell (11:2-12:2). I don't know who laid out and constructed the roads on which I drive – those planners and builders are now unseen to me, many are likely dead. Nevertheless, I see the path they've laid and I follow it.

So, overarching both of these aspects of faith – the hoped-for future and the well-traveled past – are a Creator and his unfolding plan for what he has made. These are faith's first steps: believing that there is a purposeful Creator of all that is, including our lives, and choosing to follow his purpose for all that is, including our lives. The writer of Hebrews puts it as believing that God exists and that he rewards those who diligently seek him (11:6). Now, of course, this is not some blueprint to follow with perfectly measured angles and clearly articulated dimensions. This Creator, as well as his creation, is wild and active and full of often overwhelming life and energy. This is all the more reason to "diligently seek him"! Nevertheless, we are faced at the outset with the choice of meaning versus futility, God-centeredness versus self-centeredness...faith versus sight.

In July 1999, I was with my girlfriend in San Francisco. We had been dating for almost eight months and Jamie had been under the care of a specialist at Stanford for a medical condition she had. This visit, she was going to have surgery. The evening before she was to go in for surgery, I asked her to take a ride with me over to the Golden Gate Bridge, just for a distraction. She agreed and we headed out.

We got to the Bridge just before sundown. We drove across and parked at the scenic overlook on the other side. We sat on the low stone wall that overlooks the Bay and the Bridge and we sang songs like "Sittin' On the Dock of the Bay" and "Under the Boardwalk" and we laughed. Pretty soon the sun started going down beyond the water and the lights on the Bridge came on. At that moment I got down on my knee and asked Jamie Osborne to marry me. She just stood there shaking. A bunch of tourists turned their cameras our way and started snapping pictures. I prodded the shock out of her and got her to say yes, and we got married that December. Ever since, the Golden Gate Bridge has been sort of a symbol for our marriage, and we have a number of pictures and paintings of the Bridge.

I like the symbol of a bridge. It is about joining two separate places, uniting what is otherwise divided. The apostle Paul constructs a poetic bridge to make a powerful statement about the bridging of worlds (Col. 1:15-20). It is possible that Paul is actually quoting an early creed or hymn – it is certainly begging to be sung. It is one of the deepest and most magnificent passages in all of Scripture, and it answers the question of faith: "Faith in what or whom?"

> *The Son is the image of the invisible God,*
> *the firstborn over all creation.*
> *For in him all things were created:*
> *things in heaven and on earth, visible and invisible,*
> *whether thrones or powers or rulers or authorities;*
> *all things have been created through him and for him.*
> *He is before all things, and in him all things hold together.*
>
> *And he is the head of the body, the church.*
>
> *He is the beginning and the firstborn from among the dead,*
> *so that in everything he might have the supremacy.*
> *For God was pleased to have all his fullness dwell in him,*
> *and through him to reconcile to himself all things,*
> *whether things on earth or things in heaven,*
> *by making peace through his blood, shed on the cross.*

Paul helps us gain our footing a bit after we have begun to take faith's first steps. The rather abstract "Creator-God" becomes known as "Father" here, a Father who takes us by the hand and invites us into the inheritance of the "saints of light" (1:12), those unseen ancients of the well-traveled past and fellow travelers of the hoped-for future in Hebrews. Yet this Father is not even the clear face of faith.

* * *

At this point the curtain gets pulled back. Standing behind it all is the Son of the Father-God, Jesus Christ. This historical person of blood and bone, Jesus of Nazareth, is the "image of the invisible God" in whom "all the fullness of God was pleased to dwell" (1:15, 19). So this Jesus is, in fact, God. That realization takes us miles farther along the journey of faith!

In this colossal Colossian hymn, we see Jesus in three roles – three positions, actually. First, Jesus was the Agent of the first creation, the Word of God (John 1:1, 14) who spoke all things into being when "God said, 'Let there be…'" (Gen.1:3ff). Visible and invisible, thrones and powers, dogs and dogwoods, music and musicians, seas and seahorses, love and lovers, the stars in the sky and the stars in Hollywood and even little old you and me – all created and held together by the merciful Word and Son of God. Be assured, we are not abandoned. All of it and all of us were made by him and for him, and not just on Sundays. No matter how far the world has fallen, it has never fallen out of his reach. So, we see him standing with one outstretched arm holding on to the first, fallen creation.

Next, Jesus conquered death and inaugurated the new creation. That he is the "firstborn from among the dead" simply means that he holds the primary position of authority in the new creation, the same way he is the "firstborn over all" of the first, fallen creation. (It does not mean that there was a time the Son of God did not exist and then he was born. It is a statement about authority, not obstetrics.) His resurrection is what we are ultimately about. It's why most Christians worship primarily on Sundays, each week another Easter. It's what awaits us and the world: resurrection – not clouds or a spirit-world or some home in a far-off part of the universe. Creation has been redeemed by Christ, paid for with his life, bought out of slavery to sin and decay and death and set free for life under his loving reign forever. So, Jesus stands with his other outstretched arm grasping the new, redeemed creation.

Finally, right in the middle of it all, Jesus leads the church, through which he is bringing his light into the not-abandoned world. In the poetic layout of this hymn, the part about the church is appropriately a midpoint, a bridge between the lines about the first creation and the lines about the new creation. So, too, the church in history is a sort of mid-point, a people on the way following the Way, working together amidst the remaining ravages of the sin-riddled first creation to herald and bring God's new kingdom creation. To be sure, the work of salvation was accomplished on the cross – that's the last word. But in the progression of things, the church is something of a bridge. So, there in the middle of those outstretched arms, is the church – the magnificent, supernatural-yet-very-natural body with Christ himself the exalted Head. There he stands in cruciform posture, holding together the first, fallen creation and the new, redeemed creation, with his body the church in the middle of it all. Thus, God incarnate made peace with the world by taking its sin and death to himself.

That's the answer to "faith in what or whom?" The faith that we are to be about working into our child-of-God lives, handing on to the generations, is faith that Jesus is the true Lord of all life, that God was dwelling fully in Jesus, making peace with the world and inviting us to cross the bridge from fallen and disconnected to redeemed and reconciled. Just as Jamie and I had one relationship before we crossed the Golden Gate Bridge and a decidedly different one afterwards, so becoming part of Christ's redemption, part of the church, changes us. We have his ring on our finger – the unbreakable seal of the Holy Spirit – and we live into the promise that we are destined to be united…not just for one moment, but forever. We still live on this side of creation, but we live as if we've already crossed to the other side – in Christ, we have.

It may seem a little naïve and even simplistic – faith sometimes does – but what I'm saying is Jesus is Lord. Naïve and simplistic as it sounds, this is the shrewdest and most complex truth the world could ever know. Read the Colossian "bridge hymn" again and see how all-encompassing it actually is, though it really can be articulated simply. But "Jesus is Lord" seems to be the most difficult challenge for us to live on a daily basis. Nevertheless, that is the "what or whom" of faith: Jesus is Lord. It's been said before, but I'm not trying to re-invent the wheel here.

WALKING FAITH

I wrote that faith in Jesus as Lord is the most difficult challenge for us to live on a daily basis. I wrote that because that's what you do with faith, you live it. And it's difficult because what we mean when we say "Jesus is Lord" is not nearly as simple as what so many bumper stickers and altar-calling pastors and graffiti-covered overpasses mean by that statement.

Cormac McCarthy's novel *No Country for Old Men* offers an examination of the apparent randomness and meaninglessness of life. The story is basically about a random man who randomly happens upon a random suitcase full of ill gotten money. He takes the money and spends the rest of the story running from the money's criminal claimant, a random killer who kills randomly and…well, you get the idea. It truly is a brilliant (and violent) presentation of a downwardly-spiraling world increasingly devoid of meaning and direction, where hunter and hunted are interchangeable and the questions of fate and higher law loom dark and large.

An especially tense and darkly comical moment is when the killer steps into a convenience store to pay for gas. The friendly, clueless attendant makes small talk. The killer, on the other hand, is exasperated with the man's pathetic life. He tries to get the man to recognize his own futility. Finally, he asks the man, "What's the most you ever lost on a coin toss?" The man is flummoxed, but the killer presses him. He flips a coin, covers it, and tells the man to call it. The man refuses to answer, insisting that he needs to know what he stands to win. "Everything," is the reply. The man finally calls it, and you can read the book or see the Coen brothers' film to find out what happens. But you get the point: it's all a coin toss – random.

When the movie came out, I went to see it in my Texas hometown. Again, without giving anything away, the end of the movie is, you guessed it, pretty random. As soon as it ended and the credits started, the dear, uncomplicated lady sitting behind me said flatly and to no one in particular, "Welp, guess they ran outta money." On a deeper level she got it, even though it confused or disappointed her: Was there a meaning to that? Is there meaning to any of it?

World events can, indeed, seem random. Life can seem meaningless. Questions far outnumber answers. But the truth is, no matter how things seem in our limited field of vision, life is intentional and deeply meaningful. I would dare say that if things consistently seem random and meaningless, it is because we are not telling the right story. Imagine how confusing it would be if the big bad wolf showed up in *Hamlet*, or if Harry Potter spent all his time hanging out at the bar on *Cheers* (when he walked in everyone could yell, "Harry!"), or if *Breaking Bad*'s Walter White sold crystal-meth to Captain Ahab ("Who cares about a stupid white whale. This blue meth is amazing!"). It all starts breaking down. We end up as characters in search of a story and, ultimately, in search of an author.

I know we sometimes want to shake those people who, in the midst of our tragedies, tell us, "Everything happens for a reason." They haven't any more of a clue than we have. No, we don't ever get to have all the answers. God help us if we think we do! But life begins to make more sense, or we begin to hear the music, or maybe it's just that not knowing doesn't bother us as much or as often, when we stop walking by sight and start walking by faith.

While I think one of our big problems is that we undervalue humanity and creation, it is nevertheless the position of Scripture that the unseen is more real than what is seen. First, we have our words from Hebrews, that what is seen was made by what is unseen (11:3). Then we have that magnificent hymn from Colossians, that Jesus is the "image of the invisible God" (1:15), and that "all things...visible and invisible...have been created through him and for him" (16). Those were our first few faith-steps, that there is a Creator and there is an unfolding plan, of which Jesus is Lord.

That's when Paul steps in again to help us farther along the path, stating almost matter-of-factly that "we walk by faith, not by sight" (2 Cor. 5:1-10).

Wait, what?! Nobody told me about this faith-walking stuff. I thought that was just an old expression, like "don't tread on me" or "I did it my way"...or "Jesus is Lord." I didn't know "walk by faith" actually meant something more than just hoping for the best. What exactly does the Bible mean by that?

I'm glad you asked, oh metaphorical skeptic. This faith-walking stuff is the result of being "away from the Lord," by which Paul means we have not yet been "further clothed" and "swallowed up by life" – basically, we're not in heaven and we're not resurrected (in case you hadn't noticed). We're wandering in the desert of this seemingly meaningless world where death limps through our streets, human worth is judged by madmen, and fate is decided by a coin toss. Nevertheless, the new creation has begun. God has given us his Spirit as a guarantee that we will be more alive than we can now imagine, and as much as God's Spirit can never die, so we will never die. This life is inside us now.

So, we are to make it our life's goal to please the Lord Jesus – the one who made us and all that is and who has a plan for us and all that is. Remember that God rewards those who diligently seek him. And the reward is life like and with Jesus, the one who feeds on doing the will of the invisible Father –

the one who spent his days dancing to God music and teaching kingdom songs. Jesus is the riff-master and faith is the fundamental riff of our whole repertoire. That we are living the eternal life with God now, despite how things might appear, is vital to playing with the Rock God. No matter what crazy music competes for our attention, riff-master Jesus calls us to learn the faith riff. And he invites us to play and dance with him in the midst of the madness.

KEEPING THE FAITH BY GIVING IT AWAY

I've spent plenty of time with sheet music – reading it, studying it, writing it. But if that's all I ever did with it, then what is music? Is music really music if it's never played? In this way music is a lot like love. We can read love poems and love stories. We can sing love songs and watch romantic comedies. We can even read about God's love. But if we never actually love anyone or allow ourselves to be loved, what do we really know of love? So, like music and love, the very nature of faith is that it is strongest when it is actively shared with others. At this point it may be safe in our conversation to move from faith to *the* faith, by which I mean participation in the life, ministry, death, resurrection, ascension, and loving reign of Jesus Christ in the kingdom of the triune God.

This is where so many people get off track with their "Jesus is Lord" stuff. Many folks seem to understand "sharing the faith" to mean telling you you'll go to hell if you don't "ask Jesus into your heart" or "accept Jesus Christ as your personal Lord and Savior" (instructions Jesus never actually gave per se, but the intention is usually well-meaning). In such a scheme, Jesus is reduced to Bouncer at the pearly gates, deciding who gets into Club Heaven and who's left standing outside the velvet rope. His lordship only really kicks in after we kick the bucket.

It is vital to understand that Jesus is indeed Lord over heaven and earth and the only one who conquered sin, death, and hell. Nevertheless, handing out tickets for heaven seemed to be of little interest to Jesus. He was more about inaugurating God's kingdom reign "on earth as it is in heaven," being light in the darkest places on earth, especially in our own lives. Just as Jesus is the "image of the invisible God," so he calls us to bear that same image before him and all humanity and all creation by living lives of power and purpose.

The stories are staggering, in number but especially in detail. So many thousands, millions even, who have walked by faith through the blackest nights of human history. It begins, of course, with Jesus on the cross, praying for his killers and commending himself to the Father's hands. But his innocent blood was the fountain of a faith that has coursed through the spiritual veins of quickened souls across the ages, the light of his testimony illuminating the darkest of journeys. Left to rot in dank prisons and to fend for their lives before mocking masses in arenas; burned alive, torn to pieces, hanged, drowned, shot, run through – all with songs of praise on their lips and faith, real faith, burning in their hearts. Imagine slaves, scarred from beatings, demoralized and dehumanized and treated as property, with no real chance of ever being free, picking cotton under the hot sun or maybe even allowed to gather on a Sunday, singing songs and telling stories about an unseen God whose inward presence and onward promises are the only things that lift their heads and strengthen their legs.

Far be it from us ever to have to face such dire circumstances before we begin to walk by faith instead of sight. Nevertheless, there are so many around us who have no faith, who don't know the hope that Jesus is Lord of an intentional and meaningful world and life. Even you may not have begun to let that truth have its way with you. Maybe you or those you love are caught up in the wrong story, desperate for meaning. But as the faith works its way through us, as the Creator's marred image is restored in us, as we find ourselves walking and even dancing with a living, very present God through a very meaningful story, perhaps others will not have to say they've never seen God. Maybe they'll see him in us, little strugglers exercising the power to become God's children.

The faith is lived, is given away, as God's kingdom comes. That's what it is to share one's faith. With all of our baggage, it might be helpful to call this faith, not just Christianity, but the Good News of God's kingdom. That's the faith that we're sharing. Yes, like I'm a Texan – a Texas-person – I'm also a Christ-ian, literally a Messiah-person. But what this really means is that I'm a person who is immersed in the good news that Jesus (the Messiah) announced about God's kingdom, that in his own incarnation, ministry, death, resurrection, and ascension, God's salvation promises have been fulfilled and his kingdom has come into our midst.

And so, because all authority in heaven and earth has been given to this Jesus, we follow him into the world to help others become immersed in that reality, the reality that God the Father, God the Son, and God the Holy Spirit include us in their loving, life-changing, world-redeeming fellowship... forever. What this inclusion looks like is Jesus, that is to say learning to live your own unique life according to the teaching and power and authority – the lordship – of Jesus. It isn't easy. The world is largely hostile to his teaching and his power and his authority, in the same way that cacophony is hostile to music. The order and beauty of music is an affront to meaningless noise. And the order and beauty of the faith is an affront to the meaningless kingdoms of this world. But their meaninglessness doesn't stop them from making all kinds of noise as they die. And yet...and yet, we take up our instrument, learn the faith riff, and play on – even when it seems like we're playing solo. Because faith isn't really faith until you play it.

SEVEN

THE JUSTICE RIFF: A PERSON'S A PERSON

SUPERMAN WAS ABOUT "TRUTH, JUSTICE, and the American way." What does this even mean? Does it mean the same today as it meant when the phrase introduced the 1950s TV show every week? Does Superman's justice have anything to do with God's justice? Sure, Superman was able to leap tall buildings and outrun a train, but what would Superman do with the dehumanized ones? One of the most bizarre and evil characteristics of our sin-riddled world is the plight of the dehumanized, the people who are ignored or systematically forced outside the goings-on of what most of us consider normal life. Whether because of physical or mental limitations, economic hardship, age, or most certainly political and cultural oppression, people all over the world are treated as less than human, unrecognized – often purposefully and sometimes violently – as beloved of God and bearers of his image. This is the case for AIDS orphans in Africa and for the single mom in Arkansas, for victims of the slave trade that still runs rampant even in America and for victims of a parent's abuse or a spouse's alcoholism, for regimes that employ ethnic cleansing and totalitarian brutality and for government and banking and business practices that fuel the fires of economic oppression and class warfare.

The Justice Riff

Justice is a God riff, the kind of riff that gets in your face and demands to be heard. There are things that we who follow the living Rock God should be doing about this lack of justice in the world. It's outright terrifying that he leaves so much for us, demands so much from us. There's too much to do! The world is a mess. We are a mess. When Christ returns – in 7 minutes or in 70,000 years – I don't know if he'll find us on the brink of utter annihilation or almost completely immersed in his kingdom. Either way, where justice is lacking we are closer to annihilation than to the kingdom. And the King is here now, demanding that his church work for justice in the world.

Jesus shows us a God who gets himself dirty helping others. He touches people with skin diseases and washes filthy feet and rubs a muddy spit-paste onto the eyes of a blind man and connects with a bleeding woman and holds the hand of a dead girl. Instead of joining the establishment that tries to marginalize these people, he goes to the marginalized and brings them into community. He gets all up in our messy business, because he hears our cries and he comes to us. He doesn't remove himself from the world, hiding in the trappings of elite seclusion. He puts himself in the middle of the pressing, smelly, filthy masses. This is a God who is well acquainted with the feel of a mourner's warm tears soaking through his shirt, the sounds of oppressed masses shouting in the dirty streets, the smell of booze and urine soaking a beggar.

That's how he can say, "As much as you've done it for the least of these, you've done it for me" (Matt. 25:40, 45). He makes no bones about it, minces no words – hungry, thirsty, exposed, imprisoned, naked, diseased, impoverished. There are individuals and organizations doing amazing justice work in the world, far beyond the scope of what I'll describe here. You should join them. Your friends and family and church should join them. They are only as effective as the people who do the work. But it will be utterly meaningless if we don't start with Jesus. It won't transform or last without him. But be sure, if we want to be part of what Jesus is doing in the world, we must start by standing with "the least."

FINGER WALKS WITH GOD
When I was little, my family lived on a wooded cul-de-sac in South Carolina. I was three and four years old and my dad would take me on short walks through the woods that were across the street from our house. I would hold on to my dad's finger and we would point out beautiful birds and interesting leaves and rocks and whatever else to each other. Because of the posture of my little hand wrapped around dad's big finger, we called these adventures "finger walks."

What if you could take a finger walk with God? Imagine wrapping your hand around God's powerful finger and setting out on a stroll through the woods. What would you talk about? What would you show him? Maybe you'd ask him about his plans for you, wondering if you're on the right path. Maybe you'd talk to him about your past, about the way people hurt you and the wrong decisions you made. Perhaps you'd ask about the pain and suffering in the world, maybe get God's perspective on politics. Maybe you could find out the grossest thing you ever unwittingly ate! Yes, finger walks with God would be delightful.

But what about your sin? What if God wanted to talk about all those things in your head and in your heart and in your life that maybe you wouldn't want to share with that most holy and perfect and pure One? That's the crisis the prophet Micah is facing (6:6-8). He wants desperately to walk with God, but he just can't figure out how to be good enough to enjoy a lifelong finger walk with his Lord. Micah gets all poetic and dramatic in his offers, moving from a burnt offering and a young calf to thousands of rams and a thousand rivers of oil. Finally, in exasperation at his own futility, Micah exclaims, "What do you want, my firstborn child?"

You can almost hear God sigh and say, "Are you finished?" Then his response is simple and quiet. No rivers of oil required. No sacrifices – animal or human – needed. The good path, the way of the Lord's finger walk, is clear: do justice, love mercy, and walk humbly with God. That's it. No big pietistic productions or dramatic displays of devotion on God's agenda today. All he requires is a changed life – marked by justice, mercy, and humble devotion. Simple, right?

Well, you'd think it would be simple enough – just take each moment as it comes, trusting God's lead, doing the next right thing, lighting the darkness and all that. But we humans don't seem to be programmed that way. Our nature is always to create a system of right and wrong for ourselves. This, of itself, is not always so bad. But the next step in our nature is to expect everyone else in the world to adhere to our same personal system. We start forming cliques and cults, judging others who fall short, and practicing all manner of very religious and very empty pretensions.

Jesus was surrounded by examples of such religiosity and pretension. He tells a parable about a Pharisee and a tax collector who just happened to go up to the temple to pray at the same time (Luke 18:10-14). Things are very clear for the Pharisee. He stands proudly, looking skyward and thanking God that he is better than others – thieves and rogues and adulterers. And, for good measure, he even lumps that tax collector into his list of undesirables. The Pharisee brags about his empty religiosity – fasting, tithing, and all manner of right actions that act as a Band-Aid on his cancerous heart. He has his own little system of do's and don'ts down pat. He's got it all together. He's a legend in his own mind.

It's easy for us to make such claims for ourselves: "At least I'm not like so-and-so!" We have an enormous industry of TV shows and magazines that depend on the dysfunction and self-destruction of others to make us feel better about ourselves. We depersonalize and label these humans as stars and the characters they play so we can do with them as we please. And we don't only do it with celebrities. We try our best to reduce most people to job or political party or race or religious affiliation or some good or bad aspect of their past or present. The Pharisee could have said, "Lord, I want to pray for that gentleman over there. He seems troubled. Maybe I should take him for coffee and offer a listening ear." Instead, he just thanks God that he's not like that tax collector – you know what *they're* like!

The tax collector, on the other hand, stands in a shadowy corner. He's too ashamed even to look up. He beats his chest and cries for God to have mercy on him, a sinner. Jesus reveals that it is the culturally-despised tax collector rather than the upstanding Pharisee who went home in right standing before God. Those who think they are mountains will find themselves leveled, but those in life's ditches will be lifted to lofty peaks.

* * *

Justice begins with our own standing before God: we are sinful but God is merciful. That's the key to the tax collector being set right before God – most translations say he was "justified," a vital concept in God's kingdom. There are all kinds of books to read about the meaning of justification as it relates to salvation.[3] Here I'm thinking specifically in terms of the issue of restorative justice. The justice that is happening in the life of the tax collector is the result of his acknowledging his own need, that he is "poor in spirit," and acknowledging God's provision for that need, that God is "rich in mercy." It is important to note that the tax collector must both acknowledge his need and receive God's offer of mercy. Failure to acknowledge our need leaves us bloated. Failure to receive God's mercy leaves us starving.

I don't think this is a list in Micah: *justice? check; mercy? check; humble devotion? no, gotta get me some of that*. Instead, God's perfect justice is packaged in mercy and humble devotion – i.e. mercy and humility are characteristics of God's

The Justice Riff

brand of justice. God's justice is restorative, as opposed to retributive, justice. God is a God of redemption, making all things new. What a mistake we make when we think God just wants retribution, just wants to punish sinners and teach them a lesson. The punishment of the unjust is the result of their choice not to fellowship with the God who counts himself among "the least," those who are being treated unjustly. God is not *doing* that to them, driving them away. They are running away from him through their dehumanizing idolatry. We sinners heap enough punishment on ourselves, choosing darkness instead of light. Yet the real punishment was taken by God himself, if only we will give ourselves to the crucified Christ so that he might raise us up.

On the contrary, God is about restoring. Those who choose to work for justice by restoring others to life find themselves in the company of Jesus, immersed in the kingdom reality of the Triune God. It doesn't make sense in our "survival of the fittest" culture. We want both bad and good to get what's coming. And we work real hard at fudging numbers and blurring lines to get ourselves in the "good" column. And God has no use for any of it. There are no burnt offerings we can bring, no palms we can grease or status we can attain or religious feats we can perform that will get us spiritually in the black. It's only God's gracious brand of justice, the saving work of Christ that takes each dehumanized one of us and restores us to right standing as God's children made in his image.

Think about it...justice without mercy and humility imprisons everyone. None of us is worthy of finger walks with God. He would be perfectly justified in wiping the universal slate clean and starting over. But God must have read Gandhi, who famously said, "'An eye for an eye' leaves everyone blind." No, of course it was the other way around. Jesus was the originator, saying, "You have heard that it was said, 'An eye for an eye and a tooth for a tooth.' But I say to you, Do not resist an evildoer. But if anyone strikes you on the right cheek, turn the other also….Love your enemies and pray for those who persecute you, so that you may be children of your Father in heaven; for he makes his sun rise on the evil and on the good, and sends rain on the righteous and on the unrighteous" (Matt. 5:38-39, 44-45). That is justice with mercy and humble devotion. That is the Father's heart. That is his invitation to a finger walk, because that is what it takes to be "children of your Father in heaven." We're all little ones… we're all "the least."

…AND JUSTICE FOR ALL

Imagine a scene from a documentary or film depicting the 1960s – not a specific film, just scenes in your head. In that imagining you're likely seeing the Kennedys, Martin Luther King, Jr., helicopters and soldiers in Vietnam, hippies at Woodstock, the moon landing, protesters in the streets, etc. If you're old enough you may even be seeing memories of your own life. What I want to draw your attention to is the soundtrack of your imagination. You're probably hearing Creedence Clearwater Revival's "Fortunate Son" or Bob Dylan's "The Times They Are a-Changin'," The Stones doing "Street Fighting Man" or Hendrix at Woodstock playing the national anthem, The Beatles' "Revolution" or Aretha singing "Respect" or Buffalo Springfield's "For What It's Worth" or Sam Cooke's "A Change is Gonna Come." There's plenty to choose from. What they all have in common is that they are attempts by musicians to speak truth to power. It's no wonder that such a turbulent decade would be largely scored with a soundtrack of protest music. But ever since Woody Guthrie wrote on his guitar the words "This Machine Kills Fascists," rock and roll has been about confronting soulless institutions, railing against the bloated greed and blind dictates of power.

But long before Woody, God's prophet was speaking truth to power. God himself confronted and railed against a soulless institution. The especially striking thing is, the institution the

Rebel God was railing against was that of his own people. One of the most chilling passages in all of Scripture (Is. 1:12-17) paints a picture that should be horrifying, but is lived out in churches – tragically soulless institutions – all around the world every week. Speaking through his prophet, God explains to his people that he is not interested in their worship. God even goes so far as to say that his "soul hates" their worship gatherings. He can't look at them anymore.

Can you imagine this? The people get out of their cars and shuffle up to the doors. They mingle in the narthex or foyer and find their favorite seat in the sanctuary or worship center. The band or piano or organ starts playing and everyone stands to their feet, singing a favorite old hymn or new praise song. Announcements are made, hands are shaken, people are baptized, more songs are sung, prayers are prayed, an offering is taken. The pastor stands and preaches a dramatic sermon. There's another prayer, maybe communion, maybe an altar call, more music, and the people are dismissed to try to beat the other church-goers to favorite restaurants. All of this happens…and God is completely absent.

This isn't some empty threat. God says this is a reality. It is possible that he's genuinely not interested in his people's worship. Did we take him for granted, just assuming he was always sitting there smiling as people sing his songs and preach his word? Maybe it's news to us that, just like us, God has a choice as to whether or not he goes to church. It's a little odd considering he's the one supposedly being worshiped. So why wouldn't God show up? I mean, I've heard some bad preaching and some bad singing; but so bad that God doesn't show up? So bad that God is marching in the streets, protesting the institution?

What God is rebelling against is idolatry, idolatry in the form of injustice. It's tragic in the truest sense of the word. Like the Macbeths and their "damned spot," the worshippers' hands are stained with blood. They may have the best preaching and the best music and the fanciest building in town. But there's one thing they don't have, and that's what keeps God at a distance: they don't have justice. And their lack of justice is a symptom of the disease of idolatry, the idolatry of dehumanization. That's the foundation of injustice, dehumanizing an individual or a group for the sake of marginalizing them, excluding them, persecuting them, even exterminating them. These are people made in the image of God, children beloved of God. So, whether as the result of ignorant mockery or calculated oppression, they are labeled and masked and grouped together as something less than human. And that is exactly why God hates injustice so deeply.

God tells his people to make themselves clean, to stop doing evil and learn to do good. These might sound like vagaries, those do's and don'ts that we misidentify as holiness. Fortunately, God gets specific. Being clean, not evil, and doing good boils down to one specific action here: seeking justice. God's people can sing and dance and feast and lift their hands in worship all they want. But God takes to the streets and shouts out protest songs when there's blood on those lifted hands – the blood of the oppressed, the widow and the orphan, the dehumanized.

DEAD DOG

One well-acquainted with blood and protest songs was King David, who had ups and downs like a rocket has ups and downs – soaring to the heavens only to crash into the sea. One of David's finest ups is a stirring picture of restorative, humanizing justice. Having recently secured his place of power and authority, David's tender heart is moved toward his late great friend Jonathan, whom he wishes to honor. But how? He could have immortalized him in one of his beautiful songs. He probably should have built the Prince Jonathan Memorial Hospital. The smart thing would have been to establish an annual "Jonathan Day" in Jerusalem. But David is different, a man after God's own heart. Specifically, "David

The Justice Riff

reigned over all Israel; and David *administered justice* and equity to all his people" (2 Sam. 8:15, emphasis added). Right after this characterization we find it illustrated in an especially touching and rebellious way.

David's strange scheme to honor Jonathan is to seek anyone who might be left from the house of Saul, Jonathan's crazy father and David's arch-nemesis, so David can show kindness to that descendent (2 Sam. 9).

What?! Look David, I know you're new to this king business, but you're supposed to kill all the family and servants of competitor kings, not throw 'em a party! Saul's descendants could contract an assassin or raise up an army and take you out, and you're going to invite them to supper? But that's exactly what David does.

Turns out there's one guy, Jonathan's son and Saul's grandson, Mephibosheth. During the downfall of the house of Saul, the five-year-old Mephibosheth was dropped by his nurse in her attempt to flee with him. As a result, he became "crippled in both feet" (4:4). Now he is the lame legacy of the powerful but misguided ruler, Saul. It may seem like a tragic legacy, but Jonathan's kindness to David and David's commitment to justice are about to turn that tragedy into a holy triumph.

One of my favorite parts of the story is when David and Mephibosheth meet. Little Mephibosheth, who likely thinks he has been discovered and summoned only to be executed, comes clopping in and struggles to bow to the ground before the great king of Israel. But David throws off all pretense and simply shouts, "Mephibosheth!" Mephibosheth, surely thrown by the informality, keeps his gaze averted and asks why it is that the king should notice a "dead dog" like him. But David has a plan. All the land that once belonged to King Saul will now be given to Mephibosheth. And greatest of all, lame little Mephibosheth will always have a place among the beautiful and powerful at the king's own table, where he will eat as one of the king's own sons. The last line of the story captures it all masterfully: "And Mephibosheth lived in Jerusalem, because he always ate at the king's table; he was lame in both feet" (9:13). The end.

We always love King David because he's such a screw-up but still ends up being a good king who ultimately seeks to do right by God. And his example here is certainly one that bears emulating. But you and I are as much Mephibosheth in this story as we are David. First, everyone is a child of the King (though many won't accept the honor). True justice extends value and honor to all people. David recognizes that Mephibosheth is not a worthless "dead dog," but a child of the king. Though, like David, we must extend such value and honor, we also must, like Mephibosheth, allow ourselves to be valued and honored. Second, everyone is "crippled in both feet." While we are children of the King, our honor and value derive from the King's love and grace toward us, not from our own entitlement and accomplishment. Third, everyone has a place at the King's table. That is one of the most radical aspects of Christ's kingdom message, that all the "wrong" people are invited to the feast. Yet there are no "wrong" people in the new creation, for in Christ all can become "right," new creatures. And so it goes that God's restorative justice, characterized by mercy and humble devotion, works to snatch creation's fallen legacy from the fires of tragedy and restore it to the triumph of new creation – one lame, dead dog at a time.

EIGHT

THE PEACE RIFF: US AND THEM

AND THEN THERE WAS THAT time a few years ago, after the hurricane. Jesus and his disciples are in their fifteen-passenger van driving down to New Orleans to help. Along the way they stop in a diner for lunch. In that same diner is a group of pastors meeting for a lunch prayer group. They see Jesus and ask him where he's heading. He tells them New Orleans.

"Are you going to get in on the judgment?" they ask with a laugh.

"What kind of judgment do you mean?" asks Jesus.

"Well, Las Vegas may be 'sin city,' but those people in New Orleans could give 'em a run for their money. Now a bunch of 'em have relocated up here. They're just looking for a government hand-out if you ask me. Our churches helped out at the shelters when they started getting here. Worst smelling people you ever met."

"You have smelly church members?" says a smiling Jesus.

"No, those New Orleans people. They smell bad...you know, *them*."

"Judgment, huh." Jesus picks up a menu and looks it over, then looks back at the pastors. "You think those victims of Katrina were more sinful than other people in the South, that God was judging them?" The pastors nod, though they are looking a little uneasy. "What about all the ones who died in the Twin Towers on 9/11," Jesus asks. "Do you think they were worse sinners than other Americans?" The pastors sit quietly; some of them look at the floor or at their expensive watches. The disciples just sit there with their mouths hanging open. "Well, since you seem to have run out of answers, let me tell you. The answer is no, they are not worse sinners. But you, if you don't get rid of this 'us-and-them' thinking, you're going to find yourself in a hurricane. If you don't *stop* building walls and *start* building God's kingdom, you're going to find it all crashing down around you. There's still time to do the right thing...but not much." The pastors are all looking at the floor. Jesus and the disciples decide to go eat at the deli across the street.

What is the biggest threat and disruption to peace? It is not women with grudges, men with handguns, or even dictators with nuclear weapons. The biggest threat and disruption to peace is an "us-and-them" mentality. The rest of it is the rotten fruit of that corrupted tree. I'm not talking about some war – again, whether deemed necessary or unnecessary, war is more rotten fruit. I am talking about fear, greed, materialism, bigotry, racism, classism, ethnic cleansing, and just plain un-neighborliness. I'm talking about us-and-them. It comes down to Jesus and the big picture. We can't escape the fact that Jesus overcame fear and its resulting destructive divisions with love and seeking the Father's will above all else. It might sound like an oversimplification, but only to those unfamiliar with the wrenching wounds of love and the all-encompassing demands of the Father's will.

* * *

This us-and-them story is what Jesus encounters, in a nutshell, as he approaches Jerusalem with some Galilean pilgrims and other rag-tags he met along the way (Luke 13:1-9). Folks in the crowd tell Jesus and his followers the news about some other Galilean pilgrims who had apparently gone to offer sacrifices in Jerusalem and were killed by the occupying Roman forces. It's appropriate that they would tell Jesus this news. After all, here Jesus is leading a band of pilgrims from Galilee to Jerusalem, just like those who got killed. But it's Jesus' ability to read between the lines that creates the tension in the story. Jesus perceives that what these folks are really saying is that those Galilean pilgrims got what they deserved. After all, bad things only happen to bad people and, by corollary, those who avoid tragedy must be favored by God. They think they're talking Jesus' language. He talks about judgment, that God's kingdom is coming and things will be set right, so isn't this it? What God must really want is for the Jews to take up arms against their oppressors and overthrow Rome. God's kingdom will come when the "us" defeats the "them." That's the way it always works...isn't it?

They are missing the point entirely. They don't understand what judgment is about, and they certainly don't understand the redemption that is the result of God's judgment. Jesus compares the situation with the Galilean pilgrims to an accident that happened when a tower, perhaps in the midst of construction, fell on and killed some folks in town. Neither of those groups brought their deaths on themselves. Nor did God do it to them. But then Jesus tells them something that must send chills up their spines. If they don't stop being God's people on their own terms and start being God's people on God's terms, they are going to perish the same way.

Jesus really emphasizes that: If they don't repent, they will perish *in the same way*. Many people mistakenly make this passage about hell, that if people don't choose to turn from sin and turn to Jesus, they will perish in hell. This is not what is being said here. What Jesus is saying is that Abraham's children have been responsible for bringing God's light to the world for more than a thousand years, and they have been failing miserably. Now the end is near. If they don't answer Jesus' call to true kingdom building, then they will soon find *their* blood being spilled, they will find buildings crashing down upon *them*. So, really, these ones standing in judgment are only heaping judgment upon themselves. With the hindsight of history we can see, they did not heed Jesus' call and, only a generation later – just as Jesus prophesied – Jerusalem did tragically fall to Rome around AD 70, with the people killed or scattered and the Temple destroyed. But why did they keep failing?

Us-and-them. A mentality of us-and-them goes against everything Jesus stands for, because he is about making peace and us-and-them destroys peace, he is about including and us-and-them is about excluding, he is about love and us-and-them is about apathy and fear. If loving others, including our enemies, came naturally, then God wouldn't have had to tell us to do it. He wouldn't have had to die – for us and them – to show us. But anyone can be our enemy at any moment. It happens when we see others as "them," so different from "us." Us-and-them thinking has husbands and wives fighting over who "wins" an argument or even who "wins" a divorce. Us-and-them thinking has upper classes and lower classes, white collars and blue collars, resenting each other instead of helping each other, fighting to get a bigger share of a rotten pie rather than making a better pie together. Us-and-them thinking has different ethnicities trying to keep each other in their place, however mixed-up and misguided that place is. Us-and-them thinking is responsible for countless deaths and robberies and all kinds of unspeakable crimes. Us-and-them thinking is responsible for inner loneliness and alienation. Us-and-them thinking has Dr. King's indicting words still true decades later, that 11 o'clock Sunday morning is the most segregated hour in America. How can this be true, when peace is the very nature of the Triune God, living in community and opening the door to each and all of us?

"God did not send his Son into the world to condemn the world, but to save the world through him" (John 3:17). God has not given us what we have and made us who we are so that we might keep ourselves divided from others. We have what we have and we are who we are so that we might serve others. Our spouse, our children, our neighbors, our enemies – no matter whose feet need washing, peace is made on our knees. That's what Jesus shows us as he washes the mud and dung off the calloused feet of his betrayers. If God calls us his people, it is not to show that we're right and everyone else is wrong. If God calls us his people, it is to show that God is right and the rest of us are just following, humbled to be in the family. If there is an "us and them," then it is God and the rest of us. It is only by God's grace that we are invited in.

But we *are* invited – all of us. That's what God does: he opens himself up and invites even the most despicable of us in…even me! And he tells us to go and do likewise – to strive for peace with all people (Rom. 12:18), seeing "us" in "them," until we sit together around the table of God, and us-and-them becomes only us in him.

GIVE PEACE MORE THAN A CHANCE

Give Peace a Chance. It was a song for John Lennon, a rallying cry for tumultuous times, and now a nostalgic throwback to the good ol' days and heady times, man. Like "All You Need is Love," "Give Peace a Chance" is either a gross oversimplification or a small step up a huge mountain. I'm opting for the latter. But either way, it's only a beginning. Jesus said, "Blessed are the peacemakers, for they will be called the children of God" (Matt. 5:9). I think this covers significantly more ground, because giving peace a chance is a good start. But making peace requires a lot more of us. Peacemaking is a vital skill, increasingly lacking in our culture and world. It is such a vital skill that Jesus – the Prince of Peace – commends it as a chief characteristic of God's children, nothing less than a God-riff. If this is so, then why aren't we living into the peacemaking that Jesus calls blessed?

Interesting that Jesus' instructions when sending out seventy kingdom workers (Luke 10:1-12) are to, "...first say, 'Peace to this house!'" I wonder how much better we might do in reaching others if our initial orientation is one of offering peace. How much more vital might our presence be – might God's presence through us be – if we were known for peace and hospitality rather than judgment, alienation, and divisiveness.

Jesus' further instructions seem to be to: 1) Fellowship and build relationships; 2) Demonstrate God's healing, restorative power; and 3) Proclaim the presence of God's kingdom. That's it. Certainly the message of the kingdom will cause conflict as it challenges other powers, including our own self-righteousness and entitlement. And Jesus acknowledges that there will be those who reject the ministry of kingdom peace and, thus, heap judgment upon themselves. But as much as it's up to the kingdom workers, they are to be messengers of God's peace.

There's a persistent push in Jesus' instructions not to waste time with those who aren't receptive, characterized by those who reject peace. And undergirding the ministry is a full reliance on the presence and faithfulness of God: praying for the Lord to send laborers out into his kingdom fields, living with simple provisions, relying on the hospitality of others, and proclaiming only the message of God's power and kingdom. This is partially the result of the urgency at that time of Jesus' kingdom message, but it's a message I believe is as urgent as ever. Now is the time to receive the peace God is offering. Now is the time to extend that peace to others. This life of peace with God propels the message of peace.

Later, after Jesus' death, resurrection, and ascension, we see Peter reaffirming the message of peace intertwined with the message of the kingdom: "You know the message God sent to the people of Israel, *preaching peace by Jesus Christ* – he is Lord of all" (Acts 10:36, emphasis added). The context of Peter's words is the good news coming to the Gentiles, the "them." Peter precedes that line by affirming that "God shows no partiality...," there is no us-and-them for God and, so, there must not be for God's people.

The gospel we have – as much as it is the true good news of the kingdom – is primarily a gospel of peace: peace with God and peace among people, "by Jesus Christ – he is Lord of all." This is the cross-shaped ministry of reconciliation that Paul commends to us – peace between God and the world, and peace between us and our neighbors (2 Cor. 5:16-21). It all rests in Christ's lordship. Because Jesus is Lord of all, there is no person outside of his lordship. And, thus, there is no one who should not be approached with his peace. It binds us together and should begin within the church and extend outward. So why doesn't it?

I'm sure there are a number of reasons for the church's failure to be those blessed peacemakers – racism, ageism, various cultural walls and social stratifications – but I'm going to focus on two that actually seem to be accepted as a new evangelical normal.

First: rampant individualism. Our consumer culture has resulted in individualism running amok through the church. From church shopping to church hopping to church a la carte (e.g. "What programs do you have for me?"), church has become all about the individual and has lost one of its chief characteristics, namely people living in community under authority. Someone upsets us, we leave. Leadership takes us in a direction we don't like, we leave. Expectations for growth and involvement get too high, we move on to somewhere that will let us just be spectators. And with every move, every shirk of responsibility or abdication of commitment, we lose our ability to make peace.

Thinking (ironically) in terms of military engagement, I dare say retreating, abandoning a post, or going AWOL are not the same as making peace...not the same at all. But that's exactly what you would expect from someone who puts self over corps and country. Yet we have somehow gotten the idea that self is more important than church, or that church is just a collection of interchangeable selves. While the church certainly ministers to the individual, and we would never encourage someone to stay in a destructive situation, nevertheless the church is more than the sum of its parts. We've forgotten this. So when peace needs to be made, we just take our football and go home…leaving the team behind.

Second: culture wars. The phrase says it all. In the name of values that we have been told mostly by secular media are Christian, we have been swept into a war on the culture. What hope can there be to make peace when we are bombarded with the message that we are to make war? If this is the case, Jesus' instructions might be more like, "When you engage people, first offer them peace…unless they vote for a different political party or watch different TV channels or question that this is a Christian nation or say 'Happy Holidays' instead of 'Merry Christmas.' We're at war with those kinds of people!"

As a result of this culture war message ubiquitously washing over masses of evangelical Christians, any talk of peacemaking has become synonymous with hippie-dippy liberalism and abandonment of the truth. We're told peace is downright unpatriotic (which, of course, equals un-Christian). Make war, not love! Yet Jesus' instruction to his sent ones (that's all of us, by the way) is, first, offer peace. Jesus' description of the blessed children of God is that they are peacemakers. The message of the apostles, after serving a long, intimate apprenticeship with Jesus, was about the "peace of Christ, the Lord of all." This being the case, today's church would do well to learn the peace riff, and to give peace more than a chance.

NINE

THE CARE RIFF: THE GOD OF DIRTY HANDS

CROWDS. THERE ARE DIFFERENT KINDS of crowds. There's the screaming audience at a rock concert and the "huddled masses, yearning to breathe free"; Christmas shoppers and club hoppers; football fans and freedom fighters; partygoers and protestors. Crowds can bring out our worst or our best.

Jesus encountered his fair share of crowds, and he knew just how to handle them. At the beginning, there was a crowd shouting his praises. But Jesus didn't get swept up in their hype, because he knew they were fickle (John 2:24-25). At the end, there was a crowd cursing him and shouting for his death. But Jesus didn't get swept up in their hatred, because he knew they didn't really get it (Luke 23:34). And there were many other crowds along the way. And among those crowds, there were people in need of a genuine touch.

There's a fascinating story about Jesus dealing with crowds, in which he does get swept up in a remarkable way (Mark 5:21-43). It's actually one story in two parts, with another story in between. And the stories are about three crowds and three people, with Jesus as the string that ties it all together into one truth.

PART 1, CROWD 1, PERSON 1

The first crowd welcomes Jesus. He is in the middle of a successful tour, baffling the leaders and the masses with his teaching, healing the sick, raising the dead, driving out demons, calming a storm, and hanging out with the wrong sorts of people. Finally, Jesus returns to his home turf and the crowd is waiting for him. He's a hit! But from among the crowd comes one. That's who gets Jesus' attention.

Jairus is a synagogue leader. This would make him both a religious and civic figure in his community. He might even have had a prior relationship with Jesus. He could've been one of those who had previously derided and ostracized Jesus, who drove him from the synagogue. He could've been one of those whom Jesus considered part of the problem, one of those stiff-necked leaders who kept the people in darkness. Or maybe they were mutual admirers, or complete strangers. But none of it matters in this moment. Funny how we can spout condemnation and tout self-superiority and rugged individualism over coffee, but it all goes out the window when life comes rushing in.

Even though Jairus is a powerful religious and civic leader, he recognizes the presence of God in Jesus, and he reaches out to him, breaking through the crowd and falling at his feet. This influential leader becomes a common beggar. His twelve-year-old daughter, with big brown eyes and long, skinny legs, his basketball buddy who pumps her arm when she makes a shot, his princess who cuddles with him on the couch when they watch her favorite movies, the light of his life and apple of his eye, is dying.

What does Jesus do with this situation? Whether for an enemy, a beggar, a big shot, or just a hurting father, how does he care? How does God care? Jesus and Jairus are intimately connected in the meeting of Jairus's need and Jesus' compassion. Jesus ignores the welcoming crowd to focus on the hurting individual. This personal presence, intimate connection, and compassion reveal a key aspect of God's nature, as well as an important characteristic of holy care: God's nature and holy care aren't concerned with anyone being part of a certain crowd. Instead, holy care is attentive to the authentic expression of need. As Jairus falls into the dust and grit at Jesus' feet, he is casting aside the dignity and self-sufficiency of his position and crying out, "I don't have all the answers! I'm at the end of my rope and I need help!"

And Jesus shows the personal presence of God, that God is with us. In that moment of helplessness and desperation, Jesus shows one of the most beautiful, meaningful, and important aspects of care in what he does next. Jesus goes with Jairus. That's it. Well, that's not it, but it's huge. Because no matter what happens next, we've just seen an aspect of God and his care that is a focused example of the big, biblical picture, from Adam and Eve to Abraham to Moses to the kings to the prophets to the incarnation to the New Jerusalem: God makes his place with people. No matter how helpless, hurting, even hopeless someone is, God takes them by the arm and goes with them.

PART 2, CROWD 2, PERSON 2

The second crowd crushes Jesus. He is walking with Jairus to go see to his daughter as the crowd presses around them. They don't seem terribly concerned with Jairus's plight, at least not enough to clear the way. It's possible that they have other agendas for Jesus. Maybe they're anti-establishment followers who don't like his associating with Jairus. Maybe they're part of the machinery, glad to see Jesus finally falling in line. Perhaps they're just rubber-neck bystanders who want to see how it all will play out, maybe shooting video with their phones to share on social media. But from among this crowd comes one. That's who gets Jesus' attention.

She isn't named, which is appropriate. She's a nobody. She has an almost insurmountable obstacle blocking the path of even an average life. She has been living for twelve years with a condition that causes a constant flow of blood. She has gone broke on doctors and has only gotten worse. She's unclean. Because of this, if she ever had a husband she probably didn't keep him. She likely never had children, maybe she wasn't able to. She can't even participate in the normal goings-on of community life. This issue has exercised considerable power over her life.

But even though she has no power over her circumstances or standing in the community, she recognizes the presence of God in Jesus and reaches out to him, anonymously touching his clothes. What good can this do among the press of the crowd? What hope is there for a powerless nobody in the company of a rising star and gawking masses? Actually, it is toward that powerlessness that God turns. Jesus and the woman are intimately connected in the meeting of her powerlessness and God's limitless power. Jesus overcomes the crushing crowd to focus personally and powerfully on the hurting individual. The focus of God's power toward the powerless illustrates another important characteristic of God and holy care: God and holy care aren't swept up in bullying or powerful crowds. Instead, holy care is attentive to the humble reach of the powerless. In this moment, holy care shows God already reaching back.

Jesus shows the powerful presence of God, that God is able. Faith in God is always faith rightly placed. The woman touches Jesus' cloak. Immediately, her twelve years of bleeding stops and dries up. Jesus is electrified by the powerful encounter, even though he's unaware of what exactly has happened. He only knows that he has been touched in faith and that there has been a release of power. His followers, caught up in worldly notions of power, can't understand how Jesus is aware of an individual among such a powerful crowd.

But Jesus knows. The woman emerges from the crowd and from the shadows of her anonymity. Like Jairus, the woman falls at Jesus' feet and, trembling, tells him her story – *their* story. And in words so filled with love and joy you can hear Jesus smiling two thousand years later, he says, "Daughter, your faith has healed you. Go in peace and be freed from your suffering."

Look at these words that tell us so much about the nature of God's care: daughter, faith, healed, peace, freed. Each word is so enlightening. It is especially important to pick up on the fact that, according to Jesus, it was the woman's faith that healed her. God was reaching out to her, inviting her to power, and in that triumphant moment, she reached back! She accepted God's invitation to power. Not some best-seller personal power that can be attained by following seven easy steps. This is the power of leaving behind the bullying, puffed-up crowd and reaching out to the living God, all in the desperate hope that *that's* where healing, peace, and freedom will be found. And maybe he will call us daughter or son.

PART 3, CROWD 3, PERSON 3
The third crowd scoffs at Jesus. The third part of the story begins on an appropriately cynical note. While Jesus is still speaking to the healed, freed daughter of God, some people come from Jairus's house and give him the news about his own daughter: "Your daughter is dead. Why bother the teacher any more?" The sickness won. The child's lifeless body is lying on her bed. It's hopeless, over – time for sackcloth and ashes, flowers and casseroles. Those bearing the news try to hurry things on by dismissing Jesus. What good's a healer when death has darkened the door? Unless one has gone through the agony of losing a child, one can only imagine the sinking emptiness in Jairus's gut, the warm pain in his chest as tears spring to his eyes and his body goes numb. He crumbles. But this is where things turn.

God has heard the cry of his people. Instead of Jairus reaching out to Jesus, Jesus now reaches out to Jairus. Standing by, Jesus has also heard the grim news. But he responds with typically profound words, words that both comfort and challenge with cutting brevity: "Don't be afraid; just believe." How can Jesus say that at a time like this? If there's a list of what not to say to a grieving parent, that must be at the top. But this is not some well-meaning mourner grasping for the right words and failing miserably. This is the God who goes with people. He's still standing there with Jairus. Maybe it isn't over.

They leave the crushing crowd behind, just Jesus and Jairus, with Peter, James, and John. They go to Jairus's house. Outside is – you guessed it – the crowd. They are making quite a scene, crying and wailing loudly. It's probably a mixture of family and friends, neighbors and synagogue members, and maybe even a few mucky-mucks, given Jairus's position. They've all come to hold the parents' hands in dramatic fashion, wailing into the valley of the shadow of death. Jesus confronts their drama with a loaded question: "Why all this commotion and wailing? The child is not dead but asleep."

Quickly the crowd's tears of sorrow turn to tears of laughter. "Asleep?! Who does this jokester think he is? And, say…isn't that Jesus, the miracle-working rabbi? Where were you twenty minutes ago, Mr. Healer? You could've saved that poor child. And now you're cracking jokes. Or you're smoking crack. Or you're just a crackpot. Asleep…" The crowd knows how things work. Crowds always do. Alive is alive and dead is dead. So they wail and cry with scoffing laughter. But beyond this crowd is one. That's who gets Jesus' attention.

The parents lead Jesus and his inner three to the child's bedroom – posters on the wall, books and papers strewn about, stuffed animals on the floor, a basketball in the corner. She's been lying on the bed, dead…or profoundly asleep…for some time now. Like the bleeding woman, a little girl had no standing in the community. Sure, her father was a somebody. But is that why Jesus came? Or was it *in spite* of that? Either way, even a synagogue leader can do nothing in the face of death – nothing but turn to Jesus.

Jairus and his daughter – and, for that matter, the scoffing crowd and everyone in the world – are helpless in the face of death. Jairus's daughter is intimately connected with Jesus in the meeting of her death and God's life-giving creativity. Jesus breaks through the scoffing crowd to bring God's life-giving reality to the hurting individuals. The focus of God's life-giving creativity in the midst of death shows an important concept about the reality of God and holy care: Reality is not determined by the cynicism of the scoffing crowd. Instead, holy care is attentive to the faith of those who are willing to let go of cynicism and fear and believe enough to let care come in. Maybe there's doubt. Maybe there's fear. But God's reality-creating care says, "Don't be afraid; just believe." And transformation happens for those who will follow that care all the way…even to death.

Jesus shows God's creative presence, that God is God. Only God truly creates reality. And the care we need in our lives, and the care we need to extend to others, is all about joining God in creating a new reality. Rather than a new reality we could say *real* reality, since there may only be one reality we're dealing with here. The rest seems to be either illusion or, more likely, only a fragment of real reality. Certainly death is real; people's pain and suffering and need are real. But Jesus challenges perceptions with his "the child is not dead but asleep." What did he know that the others didn't? Well, he knew enough to take her by the hand and say, "Little girl, I say to you, get up!" And she does…immediately. Jesus tells her parents to get her something to eat. The next morning she is out shooting baskets with her dad.

* * *

The thing is, Jesus wasn't just living a reality that any of us could be living. Jesus was *bringing* God's kingdom reality to bear in the world. It isn't some incantation or universal force or mystical consciousness – it's Jesus. He isn't just showing the way, telling the truth, describing the life. He is the Way and the Truth and the Life (John 14:6). Yes, in many ways he demonstrates the way and speaks the truth and models the life. But it is only by our dying and rising with him, living in the new/real reality of the kingdom over which the ascended Christ reigns, that we begin to see beyond the fragments to the bigger picture. This is where we, without any hint of disingenuous dramatics, can honestly begin to say, "Daughter, your faith has healed you," and, "Don't be afraid; just believe," and, "Little girl, get up!" And we can say these things because they are having their way in our lives. Jesus goes with us and invites us to believe. Jesus releases power to us and heals us and sets us free. Jesus calls for us to get up and become alive again. And so he, in and through us, continues to do these things wherever we go as that kingdom reality comes more and more to bear on earth as it is in heaven. That's holy care.

Now a word about those three crowds. All three are really the same fickle crowd – sometimes welcoming, sometimes crushing, sometimes scoffing. If we don't open ourselves to the personal, powerful, and creative presence of God, then we become part of the same fickle crowd. We get caught up in welcoming only the celebrated and influential, in crushing with bullies and the powerful, in scoffing with the fearful and the cynical. And in the process we miss the hurting individual. We miss the God who goes with them, the God who invites them into power, the God who creates new/real reality in their midst. And so, we miss ourselves. Because who are we but just another desperate father, bleeding daughter, dying child?

THE BIG PICTURE

A concluding image to the previous three stories might be the once-dead little girl sitting at the table eating. That's sort of the way Mark ends it. But let's do a little mental camera work. Let's pull out to the girl's house, Jairus's house, with the crowd outside wondering what's going on in there. We keep panning out to include the formerly bleeding woman, maybe going to the marketplace or to see friends and family she hasn't seen in a long time. We pull all the way out to include the shore where the crowd had gathered and Jairus had fallen at Jesus' feet. The thread that pulls this big scene together is, of course, Jesus. But one thing we might miss about Jesus if we don't stop to take it all in is this: Jesus has become unclean.

Jesus didn't lead from a distance. He let his heart break with Jairus as they pressed through the dirty masses. He was touched by and interacted with a bleeding woman. He went to and held the hand of a corpse. The dictates of Jesus' law and culture would have him remove himself for a period of ritual cleansing. He should take his place alongside the undesirables on the fringes of community. Instead, Jesus frees them from their alienation and brings them into community. He restores them to life.

Jesus shows us a picture of God getting his hands dirty. This isn't typically the way we think of God, of Jesus. But what do we think the cross is all about? In Jesus we see God making himself unclean in order to make others clean as he connects personally, powerfully, and creatively. And this is perhaps the biggest lesson to learn about God and his holy care: God's hands are dirty because he's involved – intimately involved – in our mess. Experiencing God's way of caring includes turning our desperate, messy lives to the beautiful, loving God who is right there with us in the mess – arms outstretched, welcoming us into his company, into his power, into his reality. And with him, we offer the same care to others.

If we pull our mental camera on out, that's the big picture we see – from the manger to the cross: God in the mess. But then it must go on to the resurrection and the ascension, to Pentecost and the early church, and on through history to you and me on this very day: God in the mess. God is an incarnational God who redeems our mess by joining us in it. We must be careful that we don't get too distant from the mess, shaking our heads at the unwashed masses and passing by invisible beggars and tsk-tsking at the news. Because if we pull our mental camera all the way back – and I mean all the way – we see God taking the chaotic mess "in the beginning" and fashioning all that is, and we see the Son of Man coming in final glory and revealing that how we treated those in the mess was how we treated him. He was there all along – holding it all together, making all things new, taking the mess and making it beautiful.

TEN

THE BEAUTY RIFF: ANECDOTE OF THREE JARS

*P*ISS CHRIST IS A WORK of art done in 1987 by American artist and photographer Andres Serrano. It is a photograph of a cheap plastic crucifix submerged in a glass of Serrano's urine. Do you find this offensive? You're not alone. Do you find it beautiful? You're not alone. Maybe it's a horrible, blasphemous piece of junk made only to scandalize. Maybe it's a provocative comment on the blasphemous cheapening of contemporary religion. Beauty is in the eye of the beholder. We know there is truth to this, that ideas of beauty change from person to person and age to age. But is there a transcendent ideal of beauty? If so, might even the struggle to reach this ideal be beautiful? If not, has there ever been such an ideal? Will there ever be? The journey of faith has much to teach about beauty. If beauty – true beauty – is in the eye of the beholder, then is it possible to learn to behold more clearly? And, for that matter, who in fact is the beholder?

JAR #1: BEAUTY IS TRUTH

When old age shall this generation waste,
Thou shalt remain, in midst of other woe
Than ours, a friend to man, to whom thou sayst,
"Beauty is truth, truth beauty," – that is all
Ye know on earth, and all ye need to know.[4]

John Keats's 1819 poem "Ode On a Grecian Urn" is about the ideals and perfection of art as illustrated in the timelessness of a bygone age. In the poem, the narrator is commenting on a classic marble urn from ancient Greece. The images on the urn are revealed as the poem progresses. One image is that of a man chasing his lover. Though he will never catch her, they are perfect in their timelessness – neither her beauty nor his love for her will ever fade. Another image is of a procession of townspeople, a priest, and a cow, all on their way to a religious ceremony where the cow will be sacrificed. But, again, all are immortal – the townspeople and priest, the sacrificial cow that is never actually sacrificed, and even the town they have temporarily vacated – none will ever know corruption or death.

Keats ends the poem with praise for the form itself, the urn, with its shape and adornments and timeless beauty. Throughout the poem, the narrator is in the position of considering the piece of art detail by detail. As this happens, the reader is drawn into the same position and, thus, becomes one with the narrator and experiences the art for him or herself. The sort of "meta" moment comes when (and if) the reader realizes that the larger art form being experienced is Keats's poem. So, in the end, the whole thing is a tribute to art itself and, more broadly, the ideal of beauty. Beauty is truth, truth beauty.

This, too, is something of the ideal of beauty according to the life of faith. As the lyrical creation story of Genesis describes, "God saw all that he had made, and it was very good" (1:31).

It isn't important or particularly helpful at this point to get caught up in how God made everything or how long it took. The main point is that God made it, he made it on purpose, and what he made makes him happy. He considered it to be very good and, as such, I don't think it would be a stretch to think God considered what he made to be beautiful.

What the Creation Story is really describing is the building of a temple, in which humanity can live happily with God while working in peaceful perfection as stewards of what God has made, and even as co-laborers with God in the cultivation and care of this beautiful world. So, here is a beautiful ideal: humanity in harmony with creation and Creator.

Despite our worst efforts (more about those in a minute), I don't think the Creator's joy in this beauty has waned. Have you ever been happy with a job well done? When was the last time you built something, did a good job on homework or a test, created some sort of work of art, were proud of your children or the home you and your family have made, ran a race, took an enjoyable trip, performed well at work, and so on? When was the last time you looked at something you had made and saw that it was very good? Creation is God's job well done. You know that deep joy when you stop to take in a sunset or a starry sky or the mountains or an ocean. You know the pure delight of watching a playful puppy or a flitting butterfly or a field of wildflowers or a pod of dolphins or a sleeping child. From the subatomic to the astronomic and everything in between, there is a perfect beauty that reflects the will of the perfectly beautiful Creator. This beauty points all witnesses to the Maker's beauty and artistry and creativity. But this beauty also exists in timeless and silent perfection without the need to be witnessed at all. This is its deeper truth. There is beauty in this truth. There is truth in this beauty. And we were made to know it and make it known throughout the earth.

JAR #2: A JAR IN TENNESSEE
It took dominion everywhere.
The jar was gray and bare.
It did not give of bird or bush,
Like nothing else in Tennessee.[5]

In his 1919 poem "Anecdote of the Jar," Wallace Stevens describes taking a "gray and bare" jar and placing it on a hill in Tennessee. In that simple act, the entire scene is transformed as "the wilderness rose up to it, / and sprawled around, no longer wild." The intentional juxtaposition of something simple and small like a jar placed among something vast and wild like trees and a hill creates a work of art, focusing the eye on the beauty that was already there, inherent in both. The poem seems inspired by Keats's "Grecian Urn" – another vessel used to pay tribute to the power and perfection of art and beauty.

But something's amiss. For one thing, the language itself is rather awkward. There's a mixture of the very plain, almost childlike, with the more formal and poetic. Also, the scene – especially compared with that of Keats – is comical, but there's something of a sinister undertone. The poet/narrator has done something silly by placing an ordinary canning jar in the middle of the natural beauty of the hilly wilderness. But, despite creating art by adding a focal point, the poet/narrator seems to have intruded. His jar now takes "dominion" and seems out of place, "Like nothing else in Tennessee." Compared to the beautiful colors of a bird and the lush fullness of a bush, the jar is gray and bare. Perhaps this beauty is telling a different truth.

There is a more profound beauty that emerges within the story of God's creation, appearing just at the end of the story, yet really the beginning of something new: humanity. These humans were still very much part of all that God saw and called very good, yet they were different, "like nothing else in Tennessee." God's plan for creating humanity included the caveat that, "God created human beings in his own image, in the image of God he created them; male and female he created them" (Gen. 1:27). Scores of generations later, another divinely-inspired poet would rhapsodize to the Maker, "You have made [human beings] a little lower than the heavenly beings and crowned them with glory and honor. You made them rulers over the works of your hands; you put everything under their feet..." (Ps. 8:5-6).

Though some would argue otherwise, it is true that, more than anything else in creation, humans can reason and plan and create and express and love and be self-aware and experience the deepest extremes of joy and sorrow. If the Creator's beauty is reflected and experienced in his creation – the work of his hands – then how much more so must this be with the part of creation that he made in his own image and crowned with glory and honor and put in charge of his creation? If there is profound truth and beauty in the rest of creation, then how awe-inspiringly wonderful and mystifyingly beautiful are the heart and mind and soul and strength of humanity? Indeed, there is such powerful truth and beauty in humanity that we are tempted to abandon our adoration of our Creator and focus our worship on ourselves. Tragedy of horrific tragedies, we sometimes give in to that temptation.

Humans were given dominion over the world to worshipfully work alongside the Creator in this temple, enjoying and nurturing its beauty, even as we reflected the Creator's beauty in a uniquely beautiful way. But we were also given limits. Like boundaries of form and medium and light and color give healthy limitations to a work of art, humans were given the limitation of being human...bearing the image and intimacy of the divine, but as limited humans. We didn't like this boundary. We "took dominion everywhere." The perfect beauty of humanity in harmony with creation and Creator gave way to something sinister. It upset the balance of things, breaking the silent truth of deep beauty. It wanted everything to witness its own glory. It stopped our creation work midway, so that we were left with an unfinished symphony[6] – harmony here, cacophony there...snow-capped mountains and devastating earthquakes, the beautiful complexity of DNA and the tragic mutation of cancer cells, nourishing showers and destructive hurricanes, a healthy growing child and a body whose immune system is at war with itself. As Paul described, "The creation waits in eager expectation for the children of God to be revealed...We know that the whole creation has been groaning as in the pains of childbirth right up to the present time" (Rom. 8:19, 22).

So here is a different kind of beauty. Like the jar in Tennessee, we are placed among the wilderness, a focal point for the untamed and a witness to the inward and surrounding beauty. Also like the jar, we invade and take dominion, gray and bare vessels of ugliness and destruction, like nothing else in Tennessee. And somewhere in the juxtaposition – or maybe many places in the juxtaposition – there are still glimpses of truth. In some ways, because of the struggle involved in discerning truth from lie, the truth that is revealed is of an even more profound and enlightening nature than that born of the ease of innocence and naiveté...sometimes. But even covered in mud and dung and spittle and blood, the truth is beautiful.

JAR #3: JARS OF CLAY
For God, who said, "Let light shine out of darkness,"
Made his light shine in our hearts
To give us the light of the knowledge of God's glory
Displayed in the face of Christ.
But we have this treasure in jars of clay
To show that this all-surpassing power
Is from God and not from us.

One more passage tells of one more jar. This jar exemplifies the beauty and truth of timeless perfection, as well as the beauty and truth of ugly struggle. Paul writes of the ultimate juxtaposition: divine treasure in jars of clay (2 Cor. 4:6-7). Moving beyond creation cultivation *alongside* the Creator. Moving beyond the destructive dominion of creatures enraptured with themselves. This third vessel points to something new. Here is the Creator living as one with and within the creature, as the creature lives as one with and within the Creator, though they are always and forever distinct. Some early theologians maintained that, even if humanity had not led themselves and creation into the fall, the incarnation of the Son of God would still eventually have happened, because humanity and divinity were meant to be together in the unique way of Jesus Christ.[7] Whether or not this is true (for who can ever say definitively), we can now experience a union that is beyond anything known before, or other than, that made available in and through Jesus Christ, the Son of God.

And this is the good news that is the ultimate, incarnated, beautiful Truth. Jesus, the Son of God, lived the beautiful way of God's kingdom. He took our sin and death into his own death, becoming the Way so that we could humbly rule with him in the kingdom as it comes on earth as it is in heaven. He even filled us with God's Spirit, so that we become the temple filled with the very Life of God. So, no longer is our calling only to work alongside the Creator in the temple of creation. The new dimension of this is that we, people of faith, work in intimate union with the Creator as his *temple within the temple* of creation. We, who once violated the limits of our dominion by stealing the knowledge of good and evil (Gen. 2:17), now have been freely given "the light of the knowledge of God's glory displayed in the face of Christ." Miraculous and beautiful as all this is – as we seem to be – what's to prevent that ugly and destructive self-worship we humans have always been so fond of?

Jars of clay. It is God who made the light shine in the darkness, including the darkness of our own hearts. It is God's glory we are coming to know, not our own. And it is the face of Christ, God's Son, from which the glory shines. We avoid the tragic fate of Narcissus – so attracted to his own beauty that he died while hypnotized by his reflection in a pool – by recognizing that we are not the treasure, but merely the jars. The "all-surpassing power is from God and not from us." We are the fragile vessels – the cracked pots! – within which the divine beauty shines. Yet there's a special kind of beauty that comes from the light shining through those cracks, the divine story told in our wounds. This, too, is a reflection of the knowledge of God's glory displayed in the face of Christ, as the prophet declared, "…he was pierced for our transgressions, he was crushed for our iniquities; the punishment that brought us peace was on him…Yet it was the LORD's will to crush him and cause him to suffer, and though the LORD makes his life an offering for sin…the will of the LORD will prosper in his hand. After he has suffered, he will see the light of life and be satisfied; by his knowledge my righteous servant will justify many…" (Is. 53:5, 10-11).

So this is the story of beauty: God redeems the world by becoming one of these earthen vessels, these jars of clay. He becomes dirty and weathered, fragile and cracked and, finally, shattered. And with that shattering the divine light explodes into the world. Now is the dark, dead, deceiving prince of this world driven out. Here is illuminating light, everlasting life, and the God who is Love. So this becomes our ideal, our model of perfect beauty. We too, dirty and weathered and fragile and cracked, we carry that same light, that same life, that same Love inside us. We begin again to learn and write the music of the unfinished symphony, to become the children of God that all creation is groaning for us to be. Through the new eyes of faith we see the beauty in the creation, the beauty in the struggle, and finally the beauty in redemption. This is true beauty, because this beauty is Truth.

PART III: RHYTHM

It's got a backbeat, you can't lose it.
- Chuck Berry

ELEVEN

RHYTHM GOD

I REMEMBER SITTING IN A CLASS laughing with a couple hundred other music snobs at the music college I was attending in Boston. The class was "The History of Rock and Roll," and we were laughing because we were watching Pat Boone. Now we weren't laughing just because it was Pat Boone, God love him. We were laughing because we were watching a clip of teen idol Pat doing "Tutti Frutti" on an old TV show, and he was just singing his heart out and twisting around and bopping his head…and snapping on one and three.

If you don't get the joke yet, hang in there – at least you're not on TV. The whole thing is funny on several levels. Pat has taken his lumps for being so square, so un-rock and roll, and he's taken them with a sense of humor. Just the image of him smiling while taking the whiskey of some rhythm and blues song and turning it into homogenized milk for white suburban kids is laughable, especially since most of those kids actually preferred the real stuff…or at least Elvis. I mean, this is the guy who had to be talked out of changing his version of Fats Domino's "Ain't That a Shame" to "*Isn't* That a Shame." But the quintessential exercise in missing the point was his utter rhythmic ineptitude.

One of the chief characteristics of rock and roll is that it places the accent on beats two and four, also known as the backbeat. (You've heard that word in songs like Chuck Berry's

"Rock and Roll Music" and Huey Lewis & the News' "Heart of Rock and Roll.") This is what propels rock, what moves it along. It's rooted in blues and gospel – real music of the people to which the people would clap along – and it is actually made more for participating in than for just listening to. Imagine folks sitting on a porch playing guitar and singing a more upbeat blues song. Or picture a gospel choir and the congregation shouting and singing praises. Think of slaves picking crops or a chain gang swinging hammers to the call of field hollers. In any of these settings you're likely to have people clapping along on two and four – one TWO three FOUR, one TWO three FOUR...don't just sit there, try it! And don't be so stiff, swing a little.

Try singing a song, maybe one of Pat Boone's favorites like "Tutti Frutti," and clap along – "Wop-bop-a-loo-bop, a-lop bam boom! Gotta gal named Sue, she knows just what to do..." If you have it in you then you just feel that two and four in your gut. Now try singing the same song and clapping on one and three – it may take a couple of times to do it. If you try it with a few songs (they need to be in 4/4 time) you'll begin to feel how necessary that two and four accent, the backbeat, is. If the accent is on one and three, the speed seems to cut in half and the momentum just stops. It's no coincidence that the roots from which rock and roll grew was a music called rhythm and blues. The blues gave rock and roll its riffs. But it's the rhythm that gave rock and roll its structure. It's the rhythm that makes you dance. As author and executive with MTV and VH1, Bill Flanagan, describes it, "What's the structure of the rock song? First the rhythm. You have to be able to dance to it, drive to it, or smooch to it."[8]

God is a rhythm God. He's not a rhythm god like John Bonham and Neil Peart, but a big-"G" God who reveals himself and his kingdom in rhythm. If it's true that "since the creation of the world God's invisible qualities – his eternal power and his divine nature – have been clearly seen, being understood by what has been made" (Rom. 1:20) – and I believe it is true – then God must be a God of rhythm. All of creation pulses with the divine rhythm.

There was rhythm in the very act of creation (and remember, the first chapter of Genesis is a poem, a song). It goes like this: One-Two-Three, then Four-Five-Six, then rest on Seven. And it can also break down like this: One-Four, Two-Five, Three-Six, then rest on Seven. What I mean is, Day One was the creation of day and night – Day Four was sun and moon. Day Two was water and sky – Day Five was fish and birds. Day Three was land and plants – Day Six was animals and humans. Day Seven was rest. Do you feel the rhythm? It really becomes like a call-and-response, the rhythmic cycle from the fields and the black church experience that happens between a preacher and the congregation – that's where rock gets its alternating verse-chorus-verse-chorus structure. So there's this repetition of downbeat and upbeat or call and response, the creation of a space and then its inhabitants – day and night/sun and moon, water and sky/fish and birds, land and garden/animals and humans. And then a rest to enjoy it all. Now you're swingin'!

There's an order to it all, and it's on purpose. The bigger song that the rhythm underlies is that creation was made by God for the glory of God's presence. And what a miracle that he made us to share and experience that presence in this wonderful place. It's a tragedy that many have taken this beautiful creation song and tried to turn it into something akin to the instruction booklet you get with Ikea furniture. Forget that! God created this temple and we get to worshipfully inhabit it and even cultivate it with him. That's the song. That's our rhythm. And it's the foundation of everything, including your life. It's what we're made for.

* * *

Now about that rest...That rest is vital. It's another vital rhythm. We work. We rest. We work. We rest. One of the reasons we are so out of God's rhythm is that we are missing the rest, also known as sabbath. And even when we rest, often we fill the space with so much other activity that it is anything but rest – musically speaking, we're playing in the rest, and not the good kind of playing. But for the most part we are missing the rest altogether.

If God established the rhythm of working steadily and then resting regularly, and we're just plowing right through, then we are out of rhythm – we're missing a beat. The drummer is playing four beats for every measure – one of which is a rest – and we're playing three beats and moving right on to the next measure. It evens out every now and then, but in between it's disastrous. And that rest is an indicator of maturity and confidence. An immature soloist fills every beat and every measure with a flurry of non-stop notes. A seasoned player can play a lick, rest for a beat or a bar and then pick it back up, confident that s/he still has control of the solo.

God also commanded things like a regular break from cultivating to let the land rest, and a regular forgiveness of debts to let the indebted rest. One of God's rhythms is work and rest, and if we want to walk with him we must find that rhythm, no matter what our culture tells us. We simply must stop for a day, to rest and worship and remember who and whose we are.

Creation itself moves to this rhythm. Tides ebb and flow. The moon waxes and wanes. The sun rises and sets as days begin and end. Each year we watch plants do the work of pushing down roots and breaking forth from the ground, sprouting and blossoming and bearing fruit. Then they unburden themselves of leaves and fruit (sometimes helped by us) and shrink back into a quiet rest until it's time to do it all again. Broadly speaking, even the seasons are a four-step rhythm – spring, summer, autumn, winter, repeat. And those seasons – that four beat cycle – are the foundation over which we play the riffs and music of our lives.

* * *

Even life is a rhythm. The birth process itself is made up of pushing and resting, with a final pushing forth into life and then rest. (Of course for the parents the rest quickly ends, not to be resumed until the children are out of the house…maybe.) Learning to take life as it comes, to find the rhythm of growing and aging, of experience and reflection, is vital for life as God intends it. We learn dependence as infants, play as children, independence as adolescents, vocation as young adults, family as middle adults. Then there's a plateau and then a reversal (plateau and reversal here are not descriptive of potential for or quality of life). As late-middle adults we hopefully learn a balance of family, vocation, independence, and play. Then as older adults, maybe we move a bit more toward play, though not leaving the others behind. And the final phase includes greater dependence again and then death. And physical death, of course, is a seed that will eventually burst forth in resurrection life. There are variances of course, but those who can learn the dance are the ones who find peace.

Like any dance, the dance of life depends on finding the rhythm. While rock and roll has given rise to all manner (and ill-manner) of dances, it's sufficient to say it's a music born of and made for dancing. It's the same with life. If someone can't feel when it's time to move from dependence to independence, they dance slower than life's rhythm. If someone can't feel when it's time to move from play to vocation, they miss the structure and accents of life's rhythm and even miss the music they're supposed to be contributing. If someone can't feel the move from work to family, they miss the joy of the rhythm, marching when life has become the Twist.

The rhythm shifts and we have to be ready to slow down or speed up, to find the beat and keep up during the more complex rhythms and to spin in carefree abandon during the simpler songs. And, odd as it may seem, even death is just a shift in the rhythm. For those who learned to dance, it's not so unusual – moving again from the dependence of the end of life into the play and vocation and family and rest that all characterize life in the more intimate company of the Rock God.

* * *

Through all of this, the church learns to keep time differently. In the following sections we will look briefly at the odd way the people of God learn to dance through life by annually rehearsing time according to God's rhythm. Our new year comes a month early, seemingly hidden and unexpected. While others are feasting, we are fasting. In the darkest time of the year, we herald the Light of the world. While life is greening and budding, we are learning to die. Amidst the blooming of this ancient earth we stand outside an empty tomb and witness the dawn of the New Creation. While the culture graduates and shuts down and goes on vacation, we are being filled with Spirit and new life, entering a new age and joining the very present God in new work. And at the end of it all, while national leaders destroy each other's character to get elected to political office, we are celebrating the everlasting reign of Christ the King. And then we start all over. It's an odd rhythm, a dance that brings together the rebellion and all the riffs and the backbeat rhythm of the Rock God. Those not in the dance won't really get it. Many will shout derision and even try to call the steps to the dancing ones. But they will never know. For even those of us in the dance have to learn as we go. It's improvisational – that's the point of it all.

We did not create rhythm or dance – not just the dance of life, but also the idea of dance period. It isn't just because we're bipeds that move in a natural two-step rhythm that we're attracted to dance. That Rock God – the Triune God – in whose image we're made, is a dancer. This is the way early church leaders like Gregory of Nazianzus and John of Damascus described the life and movement of the Father, the Son, and the Holy Spirit. They described it as *perichoresis*, which might be understood literally as a "circle dance." It is the interrelating of the Three, the movement outside and inside each other as independent and as one. This dancing, three-person Rock God moves inward to resting unity, yet at the exact same time is moving outward as an active trinity. And we are swept into it all.

This dancing Rhythm God doesn't need us to dance for him. He isn't interested in having little marchers that will fall in line, or puppets that will move as the strings are pulled. God invites us into the dance in which he is already eternally engaged. Like the backbeat in rock and roll, the Trinity's circle dance is one of God's defining characteristics. Rock music is music for moving and the Triune God, the Living God, is the God that moves. Just as the rhythms of creation and life require attentiveness and balance to get in step and move with the beat, so the Trinity's dance requires faithfulness and obedience to find the steps. It takes your whole life to learn to move in the circle and go with the divine Dancers. But even now, if we'll lean in close, we'll begin to hear the rhythm that is the very heartbeat of the Rock God.

TWELVE

BEAT 1: GOD COMING

THAT GOD IS A GOD who comes to his people is one of the most unique and revelatory aspects of this Rock God. This rhythmic marking of time begins with anticipation – memories of ancient longing and our own present hope for Christ's return. It continues with the incarnation, the Son of God coming in the pain and mess and cold darkness of childbirth. And, in the midst of this darkness, comes the light of recognition that this helpless infant is, in fact, God with us. But what is happening in this downbeat is the establishing of a new rhythm, a rhythm even beyond the beginning of a new year. For this God who comes – who came and who will come again – continues to come to us in every moment. And so it begins…

THE JOURNEY OF A LIFETIME
A voice of one calling: "In the wilderness, prepare the way for the LORD; make straight in the desert a highway for our God. Every valley shall be raised up, every mountain and hill made low; the rough ground shall become level, the rugged places a plain. And the glory of the LORD will be revealed…"
- Isaiah 40:3-5

I don't quite geek out like some (you know who you are), but I do love epic sagas like the *Star Wars* and *Lord of the Rings* films. One of the reasons I think we're attracted to films like these is that we love adventure…or at least the idea of adventure. For many of us, though, our lives seem tired and predictable. We long to put on armor, take up a sword, and set out on a quest. What we fail to realize is that this is exactly what the Christian life is, and Advent is the time each year that a new leg of the journey begins.

From the prophet Isaiah and on through generations, John the Baptizer picks up the call to adventure: "The King is coming to expand his kingdom into this world and into the barren wilderness of your lives. Get ready!" And so the quest begins – the quest to ready our inner and outer world for the coming King. We set out on the journey of a lifetime.

On our quest we come to the Shadow Valley. It is deep and lonely. The sun rises late and sets early. It is easy to despair here, to give up on the best and settle for whatever we can get our groping hands on. Surely there is nothing more than what is right in front of us. But the call is for the Valley to be filled. And what do we fill it with? Hope. The Valley is filled with hope as we move from darkness to light. No longer settling for just anything, we hold out for the best of things. The light begins to show us that there is something more. The King will bring it.

Then we face the Lookout Mountains. It is cool and sunny as we ascend, and from the summit we can see for miles. We see all kinds of possibilities, good and bad. We calculate all we could conquer and possess. We begin to fear all the obstacles we see. We look for higher mountains we could climb so we can see even more. But the call is for the mountains to be brought low. And what will bring those mountains down? Humility. The mountains are leveled by humility as we move from sight to faith. No longer distracted by all of life's good and bad potentialities, by the greener pastures and higher peaks, we focus on the path before us. Walking by faith allows for whatever might lie on the path, meeting what comes our way. The King will command it.

Eventually we come to the Crooked Road. We are going one way, then we are going another. How can this road ever get us where we're going? And where are we going, anyway? The path becomes unbearably rocky and we consider heading off in a new direction altogether. Perhaps this new path is the quest we should've been on all along. But the call comes to make the crooked path straight and the rough way smooth. And what can straighten and smooth this road? Holiness. Not a vain attempt at following an arbitrary and superficial list of do's and don'ts, but a focus, a movement from wandering to direction. No longer looking for easier paths and newer quests, we dig in with determination to continue on the journey of our lives. The inwardly straight, directed path allows us to make progress into the deeper country of our quest. The King will guide it.

As we move from darkness to light, from sight to faith, and from wandering to direction, a strange thing happens. Instead of looking to the horizon for the coming King, we turn and see that he has been journeying with us the whole way.

He fills in the Valley. He teaches us care and compassion and shows us that God is a God of promise. He brings us into the light and gives us hope.

He brings down the Mountains. He exercises authority, sometimes in miraculous ways, and shows us that God is a God of power. He shows himself faithful and makes us humble.

He straightens and smooths the Road. He frees us from slavery to sin, raises us from death to life, and shows us a God of purpose. He directs us to the Father and makes us holy.

But the quest is just beginning. The quest is always just beginning. In the winter of our lives, even (especially) as we leave behind this earthly life as we've known it, the quest is just beginning. We will journey no matter what. It's how we journey that determines where we're going and, more importantly, who we become along the way. In light or in darkness, by sight or by faith, haphazard or purposeful, on we march. We follow one king or another, building one kingdom or another, the barren wilderness of our lives flooded and blooming or cracked and dying. Choose this day whom you will serve....

And the quest continues as we – people of Hope, Humility, and Holiness seeking the God of Promise, Power, and Purpose – as we become so like our King that others can't help but join us in the ever-expanding, ever-deepening kingdom. We sing songs of King and kingdom around the banquet table, feasting on bread and wine – on flesh and blood. We don the armor of God, take in hand the sword of the Spirit, and we set out on our winter campaign, ever onward...until all flesh shall see the salvation of our God.

NOBODY

> *And Mary said: "My soul magnifies the Lord and my spirit rejoices in God my Savior, for he has been mindful of the humble state of his servant...He has brought down rulers from their thrones but has lifted up the humble. He has filled the hungry with good things but has sent the rich away empty."*
> -Luke 1:46-48, 52-53

Ever feel like a nobody? Wish you were somewhere else? Wish you had more to offer? No worries. God does just fine with nobodies from nowhere who have nothing. That is part of the subversive message of the Christmas story. Here's Mary, a teenaged bride-to-be from a derided small town who is about to fall in line to do her marriage and family duty – to become who the culture tells her she should be. Aside from being spiritually aware and hungry, she doesn't have much to offer. She doesn't have a lot of buying power or leadership potential, not even any star quality. "I am the Lord's servant," she tells the angel when he reveals God's crazy plan. "May it be to me according to your word."

God does just fine with nobodies from nowhere who have nothing. The world's powers don't do fine with that. They need you to stand in lines. They need you to need – to need them. But the message of Christmas is that God comes to nobodies. God comes to the middle of nowhere. God comes to those who have nothing. God comes and he fills the hungry with good things and sends the rich away empty. He confuses the proud and lifts up the humble. He notices the lowly while shrugging his shoulders at the powerful.

We can posture and preen and puff up, but God comes to who we really are. God doesn't come to the image we carefully craft or to our military might, to our x-factor or our superpower or our perfectly marketed product. God comes to our nakedness and need, to the ones hiding behind all the production value.

It's his coming that defines us – nothing else. That's the message of Christmas that can get lost in the glitter and lights and even well-intended festivities. It's all about a power-struggle that all others are destined to lose. A light came shooting through the darkness, and the darkness was left reeling in confusion and defeat. Governments and celebrities and trends rise and fall. We rise and fall. But who would notice a baby lying in a feeding trough?

Because not only does God come *to* nobodies from nowhere who have nothing; God came *as* a nobody from nowhere with nothing. This is how the world is saved.

HITCH YOUR WAGON TO A STAR
When they saw that the star had stopped, they were overwhelmed with joy. On entering the house, they saw the child with Mary his mother; and they knelt down and paid him homage.
-Matthew 2:10-11

The Magi couldn't have had much of a clue what they were getting into. Generally speaking – astrologically speaking –

they knew there was a king being born to the Jewish people. But what that really means, none of us really knows to this day. Nevertheless, they set out and followed the star. To their surprise, they actually found two very different kings of two very different kingdoms. But only one was worthy of their homage and most precious gifts. Only one…

Are you like me, restless and longing for more than the teetering, toppling kingdoms of this world? I want to follow that star to something real, something eternal. I want to find a king and open my treasure box and give him something good – the best that I can give. Maybe I'll give him everything.

Following the star, seeking out the king and his kingdom, giving my treasure – these require a fixation. Like a person who learns of treasure buried in a field and sells everything to buy that field…Like a person who loses something precious and turns the house upside down to find it…Like a merchant who finds the best of the best and gives up all else to have it… Hand to plow, no looking back.

There's a leaving behind. One kind of king, rather than rejoicing in the birth of the long-awaited Anointed One, instead hatches in his darkened mind a plan to kill this threat to his own power, slaughtering scores of innocents in the process.

That king is the world, digging in left and right heels of greed and power; tightening left and right grips of lust and fame. Breathing violence and destruction in the names of tradition and progress. That king is me, building an inner empire of fear and anger and defensiveness and hurt. Smearing the mortar of pride upon bricks of selfishness.

But the king that I seek is elusive. He doesn't surround himself with pomp and banners, with yes-men and sycophants. His kingdom is in the slums and ghettos outside glittering power centers. His kingdom is in the shadowy recesses of self.

One moment he's sleeping under a star, the next he's sleeping in the hull of a storm-tossed boat. "Wake up!" I cry with the fishermen. But then he's ahead of me, urging me up a hill to see his brilliant radiance, the intersection of heaven on earth. And then he's slumping up a hill to become the intersection of hell on earth. Then he's above me, urging me onto a cross and into death's dark mystery.

How badly do I want him? What is it to give him everything? It is to say I work this way and treat others this way and even think and feel this way – not that way anymore – because of this king. It is to say that my life is no longer my own, that it is no longer I who live but the king…the king. It is to know at my core, in what he calls my "heart," no matter how dark or fearful, he is there – a brightening light revealing the silhouette of a kingdom that has been there all along.

And so, treasure box under my arm and skyline of all that is familiar getting smaller behind me, I follow that star.

THIRTEEN

BEAT 2: GOD DYING

THE SON OF GOD CAME completely in flesh, immersing himself without exception into the human experience. This included growing up, family life, learning and practicing a trade, being part of a community, and pursuing God and God's will. This also included temptations to sin, the highs of acclaim and lows of rejection and betrayal, indescribable mental and spiritual and physical suffering and, finally, death. And just as God's coming was multi-faceted, so God's dying has many layers of meaning. In fact, like the rest of us, God's dying begins with God's coming. But, unlike the rest of us who put off acknowledging death's reality with increasing skill from generation to generation, Jesus' life story is told from the perspective of his death. It seems, with his words and actions all about the kingdom of God, he is actually talking about some kind of dying. In many ways Jesus' life is about death. But, of course, he doesn't stop there.

TEMPTED AS WE ARE

Then Jesus was led by the Spirit into the wilderness to be tempted by the devil.
- Matthew 4:1

Jesus: *You're here to trick me.*

Satan: *Trick you? To love and care for a woman, to have a family? This is a trick?...What arrogance to think you can save the world! The world doesn't have to be saved. Save yourself. Find love.*

Jesus: *I have love.*

- *The Last Temptation of Christ* (film)[9]

When I was about seventeen, the movie version of Nikos Kazantzakis's 1951 novel *The Last Temptation of Christ* came out. There were uproars and picket lines at movie theaters all over the country. My hometown was no different. Nevertheless, being the rebellious and curious teens that we were, some friends and I decided to go see the movie. We were relatively intelligent kids, Christians who took our faith seriously and who were also lovers of good films. Plus, of course, we loved a good controversy. So this seemed like a prime opportunity for the likes of us.

We showed up at the theater and, sure enough, there were the picketers – churchy people with bullhorns and signs. "That's not Jesus up there on that screen!" they shouted.

"Of course not," I muttered. "It's Willem Defoe…he's an *actor*."

My friend Thomas got up in the face of the chief bullhorn guy, but all either could hear was his own shouting. I asked one lady if she had seen the film. She had not. I couldn't understand how she could protest something she knew nothing about. And even if she had seen it, I had the right to see it too, to make up my own seventeen-year-old mind. After the rush of the shouting and controversy, we went in and saw the movie. So what was all the shouting about?

Well, as the name implies, in the movie Jesus is tempted. He struggles with his call as Israel's Messiah. I think that struggle was bothersome to people. He goes to the wilderness and confronts Satan. But there is another time of temptation which is what had people in such an uproar. Scripture says that, after the time of temptation, the devil left Jesus until an opportune time (Luke 4:13). Well, according to Kazantzakis's book and Scorsese's movie, the opportune time was when Jesus was on the cross.

Spoiler alert! As Jesus hangs on the cross, a little child comes up and tells him that she's an angel. Jesus has done enough, she says, and he can come down now. He's shown the world what real devotion to God looks like, and now it's time for him to settle down into a more peaceful and happy life. So, he does come down, settles down as a carpenter married to Mary Magdalene – there's a scene of them having marital relations, which is what disturbed so many people – and he lives a "normal" life. Then, when Jesus is an old man on his deathbed with Jerusalem being sacked by Rome and humanity without hope, the little child comes to him again and he realizes that she was really the devil. He had failed in his mission to save the world. Then it zaps back to him on the cross and we realize it was only a temptation – "the last temptation of Christ."

Why do we have such trouble with the idea of Jesus being tempted? We treat Jesus' desert confrontation with the devil as sort of the first temptation of Christ, though it seems likely he was probably tempted plenty of times before this, though perhaps not as severely and purposefully. But do we think that wilderness time was also the *last* temptation? And what do we think is going on when scripture says Jesus was tempted? Do we think he just strolled along in the park with temptations buzzing lazily around him like a few bothersome gnats? Why wouldn't he be tempted with marriage and sex and children and a "normal" life? And why wouldn't he be tempted not to be the Messiah and not to endure the agony of the cross and its hellish death and darkness? We actually know that he was tempted, in the garden when he told the Father outright that, if possible, he'd let the cup of death pass on by him this time. Seems like temptation to me. Yes, there's some weird stuff in *The Last Temptation of Christ*, plenty of stuff that is theologically

Beat 2: God Dying

off, maybe even heretical. But I think the tempting of Jesus is getting at something we need to understand.

Scripture says about Jesus, "For we do not have a high priest who is unable to sympathize with our weaknesses, but we have one who has been tempted in every way, just as we are – yet was without sin" (Heb. 4:15). Are you tempted by money, sex, power? So Jesus could easily have been. And, again, I don't think it was just a fleeting thing. He was "tempted in every way just was we are." So the temptations were probably like (please allow me some liberty here), "This itinerant teacher gig is shaky. I'm a pretty talented guy and it's time for them to show me the money!" Or, "Maybe it would be nice to settle down with a wife and kids. All my brothers and friends are doing it. And I really would like to have that special relationship." Or, "Look at all these people beginning to follow me. I'm a red-blooded Palestinian man. I could really unseat the authorities and take over around here." What's the point of Jesus being sinless if there was no real temptation to sin? No, I think his temptations were perhaps more real – more *tempting* – than anything we can imagine. But he did overcome, and that's the point.

* * *

I think we have two primary reasons for being so uncomfortable with the thought of Jesus being tempted. One: we think it makes Jesus somehow "less" God. Could God really have those wicked thoughts like I do? What does it say about him if he is even aware of such things? For one thing, do we really think he doesn't know about sin, that he's just somebody's little church-going grandmother with white gloves? (And even those church-going grandmothers might surprise you!) And another thing, God certainly has those thoughts when he's also 100% human. Again, that's the point. He doesn't just stand *over against* sin. He stands *with us* in the midst of sin. I certainly don't mean he wants to indulge in such things. Having a thought and entertaining a thought are different. And acting on the thought is different still. I simply mean he isn't surprised by even the most depraved of our thoughts and actions. Troubled? Saddened? Yes. Surprised? No.

The other reason we're uncomfortable with Jesus' temptations – and I think this is the main one – is that it lets us off the holiness hook if Jesus wasn't really tempted. We think, "Well, of course Jesus didn't sin. He was God! It's much tougher for me." But it's not only Jesus' divinity we're dealing with here; it's Jesus' humanity. He was tempted as a child, as a teenager, as a young career man, and as a successful leader. He was tempted in his vocation as the Messiah, tempted not to walk the way of suffering. The difference is he never gave in. We must understand: the temptation is not the sin. He peered into the inviting maw of disobedience and decided following the Father was better.

So, as soon as Jesus is baptized and affirmed by the Father as his beloved Son with whom he is well pleased, he is driven by the Spirit into the wilderness for the purpose of being tempted – the Lion thrown to the lion, if you will (Matt. 3:13-4:11). His resistance to temptation toughens and confirms him, makes him stronger in the face of the daily temptations, and ultimate temptation, that will come his way. He removes the masks of riches and flesh and power, the masks of fear and judgment and, ultimately, even the mask of death. And he finds his true self underneath it all – naked, vulnerable, completely dependent upon the Father. And in the powerful love of the Holy Spirit he learns to rest his life in the Father's hands. After that, there is no power or temptation that can pull him away. The key to it all is this: *Jesus dies before he dies.* And the good, troubling news is, he calls us to do the same (Luke 9:23-25).

The season of Lent, for example, is a time when we examine the temptations in our lives, when we too learn to let go of our own reliance on misguided ideas of worth and pleasure and power. Lent is a time in the wilderness – forty days, a la Jesus – when we fast and pray and remove masks. With the ash of repentance and death on our brow, we set out for the wilderness. But such letting go and unmasking needn't be reserved for a certain time of year. Weekly, even daily, we can train and strengthen ourselves, walking watchfully and looking back at where we've stumbled. And why?

Well, look at what happens to Jesus *after* the tempting. His cousin and ministry forerunner John the Baptizer gets arrested (and, later, scandalously beheaded), opening wider the need for someone to pick up John's call to repentance and proclamation of the coming of God's kingdom. And that's exactly what Jesus does. He goes to Galilee and begins his ministry of proclaiming and embodying God's kingdom. And he does all of this on the way to the cross. The path doesn't necessarily get smoother for Jesus after he learns to let go. His life is even more vulnerable now. But he has already died and is now alive to the Father.

We are in what can sometimes be a daily wilderness, faced with our temptations and sins. But the key thing to remember is what got Jesus through. It's the same thing that led him there to begin with: the Holy Spirit. This Spirit has just descended upon him like a dove. Then the Spirit drives him into the wilderness to be tempted. The Spirit was with him through it all. And the exact same Spirit is with us. He resisted temptation because he was confirmed as God's beloved Son and because he had God's Spirit with him, inside him, affirming his loving union with the Father. And this is true for you and me. We are God's children, beloved of the Father, and the Holy Spirit lives in us and draws us into loving union with God.

Jesus was a man who hung out at the temple even as a kid, who studied and memorized scripture, who kept his flesh in check by fasting, who got up early to pray, who leaned on close companions. And so can we – church, scripture, fasting, prayer, and brothers and sisters of faith. And Jesus was a man who resisted temptation and overcame sin. And so can we. The dance of the Father, Son, and Holy Spirit is not exclusive. We were made to live in their midst, to live as our true selves in that vulnerability and dependence and power, if only we will see. We simply must, because our next temptation will likely not be our last temptation.

SAY IT AIN'T SO, JESUS!
The next day the great crowd that had come for the Festival heard that Jesus was on his way to Jerusalem. They took palm branches and went out to meet him...
- John 12:12-13

It's springtime as I write this, and coming up soon is one of my favorite days of the year. Of course Easter is most important. And another birthday will be here in a couple of weeks, much to my shock and awe. But somewhere in this grouping of momentous spring days is Opening Day for Major League Baseball! Somebody, Leo Durocher or Wes Westrum, said, "Baseball is like church: many attend but few understand." It may be overstating it a bit, but I think this captures the way some of us feel about the game. We have certain ideas about baseball – its purity, its poetry, its near perfection – ideas that lead us to feel gravely disheartened by steroid scandals, hot-shot players who don't sign autographs and have no team loyalty, references to football as America's national pastime (though, yes, I do get excited about fall football), the clank! of aluminum bats, and for some of us even designated hitters.

Such reverence for the game was at its height in the first half of the twentieth century when, back in 1920, it was discovered that several members of the Chicago White Sox took money to throw the 1919 World Series. Among those accused was Shoeless Joe Jackson. He took the money, later said he'd tried to give it back twice, and the debate continues

Beat 2: God Dying

over whether or not he actually did anything to throw the World Series games. He was acquitted of criminal charges, but was suspended from the Majors for the rest of his life. He was a gullible, illiterate hick from South Carolina, but was such a genius in the game of baseball that even Babe Ruth admitted to copying his swing and called him the greatest hitter he ever saw. During the trials, it was reported that as Shoeless Joe was exiting the courthouse, a little boy in the crowd pleaded, "Say it ain't so, Joe!" Years later, Joe said that a Chicago sportswriter made the story up, and that if it had happened, he would've said it wasn't so, because it wasn't. Nevertheless, the story and quote live on in national mythology as a tribute to the loss of innocence and fallen heroes.

Most of us go through similar disappointments with our idols. I grew up idolizing Eddie Van Halen. I had posters on my walls, tape all over my guitar, and I even had my mother sew patches all over my jeans to look like Eddie's. I spent many hours in my bedroom, amp cranked, tapping feverishly on my guitar's fretboard, sweat dripping onto the body. But following Eddie over the years, as he and his brother Alex circle the wagons and kick one member after another out of the band, I've found myself not necessarily wanting to share the stage with them (not that the phone's been ringing or anything). I think he was better on my bedroom wall, smiling and jumping and just being a packaged hero.

Whether celebrities or people we know and admire, something often happens that knocks them from the pedestal we've placed them on and we're left pleading, "Say it ain't so!" Sometimes people are just hypocrites, but many times it's our own fault for not really paying attention or letting them be real. This is what happens on many levels to Jesus in the week that begins with celebration on Palm Sunday and ends with him dead by Good Friday.

Jesus has finally made his way to the Jerusalem suburbs, hung out and eaten with his dearest friends – Mary, Martha, and their brother Lazarus, whom he had recently raised from the dead – and a buzz has been generated in the city that Jesus and this Lazarus are coming to town. So, Jesus and his entourage – imagine we're part of the entourage with Jesus – we get to the city and here's the scene. First, the crowd is chanting in the distance. We hear them chanting "Hosanna!" (literally "Save now!") and words from Psalm 118, so we join them. "Save us, we beg you, O Lord! Blessed is the Savior who comes from the Lord!" Jesus is the Hosanna-Savior.

Next, we see the crowd waving palm branches. We know this is part of our custom to welcome the return of a conquering general. Only a few generations before, Judas Maccabaeus had conquered the pagan leader Antiochus Epiphanes, who had oppressed the people and worshiped false gods in the Temple. Judas Maccabaeus had conquered the pagan armies, cleansed the Temple, and the book of 2 Maccabees describes his return like this: "Waving beautiful palm branches, the people offered hymns of thanksgiving to him who had given success to the purifying of his own holy place" (10:7). We remember this victory every year at Hanukkah. So, this Jesus is not only the Hosanna-Savior, he is also the Conquering Hero celebrated with a parade of palm branches.

Then, we turn and look at Jesus. There he is, the Savior and Conqueror sitting on a little donkey. It seems familiar, but only later would we remember that this was all prophesied by Zechariah (9:9-10) when he said that the King of the Jews would come triumphant and victorious, yet humble and riding on a donkey's colt, and he shall command peace to the nations and his dominion will be from sea to sea! Sure enough, there he is, the Hosanna-Savior, the Conquering Hero, and also the King of the Jews riding humbly into the holy city to establish his kingdom and to claim victory over all our enemies. And if we needed any more proof, there's Lazarus,

Beat 2: God Dying

the one we all knew as dead for four days, now marching next to Jesus who raised him. But behind the twinkle in their eyes, they seem troubled. What can possibly go wrong on a day like today?

All the little people are there, rag-tag and smelly and helpless and hopeful, heralding Jesus and praising God because of the miracles they have seen. But the most powerful, amazing, praiseworthy miracle of all is the one everyone will walk away from. One of the greatest miracles in all of human history – one of two particularly noteworthy miracles over the coming days – is the Son of God giving up.

* * *

Across town is another king, whose reign is about power and wealth and the approval of others. Every year at this time he stages a parade where he comes riding into town on a warhorse, surrounded by soldiers, all to show the power of the empire. And here is Jesus, this king of heaven and earth, coming from the other direction, riding in his inauguration parade on a donkey...a borrowed donkey. He's going to stir up a bunch of trouble, challenging these other rulers – *all* other rulers, really. They're going to arrest him and beat him. And he's going to look them in the eye and essentially say (to borrow the words of Obi Wan Kenobi to Darth Vader), "You can't win. Strike me down and I will become more powerful than you can possibly imagine." Then he's going to let go...and they're going to kill him.

And that's the miracle: God gets killed, so that he can save his killers. We thought he was a conquering hero, *our* kind of hero. But where's the flash – the throne, the castle, the carefree life under the King's protection? Tortured and publicly executed? Shamefully made an example of for any would-be followers? Say it ain't so, Jesus!

No, there's no "Blessed is the Savior who comes from the Lord!" being shouted by the crowd now...just sadistic blood lust and vile derision: "Crucify him! We have no king but

Caesar." Maybe it's a different crowd, with Galilean pilgrims on Sunday and local Jerusalemites on Friday. Maybe they're just confused, not real clear on what Jesus' message really is. But they end up becoming part of the same crowd, turning from one hero to another. It's because they have no idea what power is. They are impressed with the gold and armies and oppressive control of the worldly powers. They're so impressed with worldly power that they hope they'll get a piece of it – money, fame, control. They don't want the kind of power Jesus has to offer.

The choice comes to each of us: Do we stick with the parade Jesus all the way through to the dead Jesus? Or do we look at the bloody, defeated mess and say, "Uh, nevermind... We have no king but Caesar. And I'm just trying to get a piece of his pie." If that's the choice we're making with our life, so be it. But we should know that Jesus says to that life of grasping at control, "You can't win. It dies with you and you're already as good as dead. Real power is not in grabbing more, but in letting go."

If you want to know real power, you get the donkey. Why? Because the Lord has need of it (Matt. 21:1-3). You'll hear the voices inside and out saying, "You've got to be impressive. You've got to be successful. You've got to get what you want *and* have more than your neighbors." But you'll also hear Jesus saying, "Go get the donkey. I have need of it." You follow him every day, taking up a cross, dying to yourself, letting go and finding his life flowing through you. Live in the moment. Pay attention. Give what little you have...because the Lord has need of it. You'll discover more power than you ever imagined – the power of letting go. The world will say it ain't so, that there is no such power. Even some of the church will say it ain't so, that Jesus is indeed our kind of hero – of our race and our politics and our way of thinking. But Jesus sits on the donkey – the donkey that you brought – and begins the final journey to the cross. He will come face to face with ungodly power…and he will say it ain't so.

GOING OUT ON A HIGH NOTE

Jesus replied, "The hour has come for the Son of Man to be glorified. Very truly I tell you, unless a kernel of wheat falls to the ground and dies, it remains only a single seed. But if it dies, it produces many seeds. Those who love their life will lose it, while those who hate their life in this world will keep it for eternal life. Whoever serves me must follow me…"
- John 12:23-26

For most of us, it's pretty important to leave a legacy of success. We want to be remembered for having reached the top of our game, gone as far as we could. We want to end on a high note. This was the case – for a brief, selfish moment – in the life of that great underachiever, George Costanza, from TV's *Seinfeld*.

George, of course is sort of a classic loser who has little chance of success and respect. One episode, George is in a meeting at work and he accidentally says something funny. George's co-workers all laugh and pat George on the back. But then George follows it by a bad joke and they all groan. Later, when he's telling Jerry about how he blew it, Jerry tells George about an important rule of show business: going out on a high note. When you've hit 'em with the good stuff, get off the stage and leave 'em wanting more. George adopts this in subsequent meetings and social situations. He's hanging out with friends or he's at work and he tells a good joke that gets everyone laughing, so he stands up and says, "All right, that's it for me! Be good, everybody," and he leaves, going out on a high note.[10]

This may work with comedy, but for most of us this becomes a sad trap when applied to life's ambitions. First, we define success by people wanting us. So we can easily fall into cycles of living for the approval and whims of others. Second, we never really know what the cut-off is. What is enough? It might be a good habit to be able to get to a healthy stopping point and move on. But our whole culture is geared to tell us always to want more. The high note is always just out of reach.

There's this certain point where Jesus hits his high note, at least in humanity's misguided perspective. He has spent some time with his best friends Mary, Martha, and Lazarus. And then he paraded into town with everyone praising him and hailing him as the conquering hero. Now, that same Sunday, he's at the great Passover festival with his apostles and friends and the other thousands of celebrants. It's party time! Maybe Jesus will make some more of that great wine.

He's so much the life of the party that some Greeks are looking for him. These Greeks were likely "God-fearers" – Gentiles who revered and even prayed to the God of the Jews. They would have come from surrounding territories to the Passover festival to join in the worship and celebration. There was even a walled-off outer court in the Temple for the God-fearers. The point is, they weren't local and they weren't Jewish, yet they come to Jesus' disciple Philip – maybe they knew him or maybe because of his Greek name – and they ask to see Jesus. Philip goes to Andrew and they both go and tell Jesus. And what is Jesus' response? "All right, that's it for me! Be good, everybody."

Seriously. Jesus says that the hour has come for him to be glorified, to end on a high note (which, of course, is simultaneously the lowest note in human history). Now, if you didn't know the rest of the story, you'd think what Jesus means by being glorified is that now his ministry is going to explode. The Greeks have heard about him and are coming to meet him. No more of this local stuff – it's time to go global. And, in a sense, that's exactly what Jesus means. But, as is typical with Jesus, what that looks like is very different from what we'd expect.

Beat 2: God Dying

First, for Jesus, being glorified means obedience to the Father, even to the point of death – *especially* to the point of death. As soon as Jesus hears about the Greeks, he says that the hour has come for him to be glorified. And then he immediately defines what that means with a parable, saying that a grain of wheat must go into the ground and die in order to be fruitful. And this is just hunky-dory for Jesus, right? Jesus is perfectly content just to cruise along, crystal-clear and happy about God's will for him to die, right?

Listen to what he says about it as he prays right in front of everybody. "Now my soul is troubled. What do I say? Father, save me from this hour. No! It is for this reason that I have come to this hour. Father, glorify your name." And then, a miracle… Unlike the other Gospels, in John's telling, we don't hear God's voice at Jesus' baptism; and there is no account of the Transfiguration where, in the other Gospels, we again hear God's voice. But here, in the midst of Jesus' troubled soul and struggle to remain faithful, this is the moment the Father speaks so powerfully the bystanders think it was either thunder or an angel. This is the moment the Father affirms that Jesus has glorified him throughout his ministry, and will glorify him all the more in his upcoming death. So, the true breakthrough and true glory lie in obedience to the Father, to the point of death.

The second unusual way Jesus ends on a high note is in the way his ministry goes worldwide. First, the grain of wheat must go into the ground and die. But as a result of that, it bears much fruit. That's where you and I come in. For Jesus, being glorified also means his *followers* must be obedient to the Father, even – and *especially* – to the point of death. If Jesus becomes a rock star, then that's it, his reach only extends as far as his own arms – he remains a single grain. But if he does something much bigger, like taking our God-blocking sin and death into the ground and killing it, then his reach explodes and extends to and through each of us. We are the fruit of his broken, dying, life-giving seed. His light will shine and his words will echo across the ages, being spoken to and through each of us. His very presence will remain until the end of the age. And it's all summed up in a new command...punctuated by death.

A NEW KIND OF LOVE
A new command I give you: Love one another. As I have loved you, so you must love one another. By this everyone will know that you are my disciples, if you love one another.
- John 13:34-35

My cousin Andy and I used to get into all sorts of trouble when we were kids. It wasn't that we were setting fires or anything (well, not big fires). It was more like the time we disappeared for a while into the piano room at our grandparents' house. We eventually emerged with scissors in our hands and our hair butchered beyond help, and we proclaimed proudly, "We cut our hair!" Or, when we were a little older, sneaking out of the house for a late-night adventure, only to find the door we had taken care to leave open for ourselves locked up tight. It was drawing on furniture, tying granddaddy's shoelaces together, bringing horned toads into the house, etc. The fact that this sounds familiar to most of you is why the words, "I want you to be on your best behavior" also sound familiar. Whenever parents are going out and leaving their kids in the care of a baby-sitter, they always have to tell the kids to be on their best behavior. Or when the family is going to be in public – at church or a restaurant or shopping – the kids are to be on their best behavior. Or playing in the yard or going to school or sitting home watching TV or whenever....We always want our kids to behave a certain way to ensure them the best of life, and also to represent the best of our family.

Right before the end, Jesus has a similar moment with his closest followers. Judas has just walked out into the evening, into his destiny as Jesus' betrayer. The door shuts behind him and you can almost hear Jesus catch his breath. Things have just kicked into high gear and Jesus knows the end is very near. He turns to his disciples and tells them, "I'm going out, and I want you to be on your best behavior while I'm gone." You can actually hear the stern but loving tone in his voice. He gives them a "command" but he calls them "my children." He knows their foolish hearts and their shaky faith, but he also knows that they're *his* children and, as he will tell them, he is not leaving them alone – the Spirit will fill them and lead them. But they must choose to love. We commemorate this in what is called Holy or *Maundy* Thursday, from the Latin *mandatum* for "commandment," from which we also get our word "mandate." And so this is Jesus' mandate, his new command (John 13).

Love. Jesus calls this command to love one another a "new command." But even way back in Leviticus the Jews had been instructed to love their neighbors (19:9-18). What's so new about Jesus' command? It's not just the command to love one another that Jesus is springing on the world here. It's the style, the nature of that love that is fresh. Jesus adds the instruction, "*As I have loved you*, so you must love one another." Jesus has been with these people for a significant amount of time, healing and teaching and forgiving and serving. Just a few minutes ago he shared a deeply meaningful meal with them – his last meal, the elements of which he declared to be his very life that they should repeatedly take and affirm inside themselves. Then he knelt down in front of each of them – including Judas – and washed the dirt and dung from their calloused feet. And in just a few hours, he will watch most of them run away and hide as he hangs naked in public shame as the embodiment of God's love for each wretched, beloved one of his children. "As I have loved you, so you must love one another." This is, indeed, a new kind of love.

But, as usual, Peter misses the point and acts like a doofus. This is why so many of us identify with Peter, because we're all doofuses at some time or another. Jesus has just laid out this thing about a new command to love one another with Christ-like love, and Peter says, "Whoa, wait a minute...what was that part about leaving?" Jesus has been telling them all along that he must be handed over to the authorities, be crucified, and on the third day he would rise. They've just had the last supper where Jesus declares the bread and wine to be his body and blood given for the world. Jesus says that one of them is about to betray him, and Judas – a known crook – has just stormed out into the night. And Peter says, "What's going on? You didn't say anything about leaving!" And then, like a little kid, Peter says, "Can I come?...Please, please, please!" Jesus tells him that he can't come now, but he will be there later (a dubious promise). Then, to add insult to the whole clueless incident, Peter says maybe the dumbest thing he's ever said – which is saying a lot. Peter says, "But...I will lay my life down for you." All the air gets sucked out of that upper room for a minute. Everyone looks around at each other, listening for a pin to drop. Then, after excruciating silence, Jesus says, "Peter, will *you* really lay down *your* life for *me*? Careful about making those hasty promises."

Our feeble grasp on love often has us making hasty promises. We make marriage vows, clueless about what will be required of us day by day for fifty or sixty years of faithfulness. We bring children into the world unaware of the love required to get through the sleepless nights of infancy, the sleepless nights of adolescence and the teen years, and the sleepless nights when they move back home after college. Somehow our kids are as flaky and fickle toward us as we were toward our parents. This is largely the result of the fact that our understanding of love has to grow through years of marriage and parenting, but the kids are just getting started.

And what are those things we learn about love, about that Christ-like love that he likens to a bridegroom with his bride?

Consistency, for one. Christ-like love is consistent. Jesus warns Peter about making rash promises because Jesus knows that Peter's love is inconsistent. He will promise to follow Jesus to death out of one side of his mouth, but will soon deny Jesus three times out of the other side of his mouth. Christ-like love keeps moving forward. It is a pilgrimage that meets each day with the resolve to remain obedient to God no matter what distractions or temptations challenge us along the way. Christ-like love is what pastor and author Eugene Peterson (appropriating Friedrich Nietzsche) describes as "a long obedience in the same direction."[11] No matter how exhausted or harangued or even abused Jesus was, his love remained consistent – facing the cross, forgiving his executioners, and dying on behalf of humanity's worst.

Also, Christ-like love is caring. It sees the need in the other and it seeks to meet that need at the expense of self. It is caring as it stops to answer the cries of a filthy beggar. It is caring as it stoops to wash the feet of a murderous betrayer. It is caring as it steps onto troubled waters to pull up a drowning backstabber. Christ-like love trains our eyes to see the need and hurt in others no matter how it got there or what they've ever done to us or not done for us. This kind of care might also be described as redemptive. It sacrifices itself to free another from bondage.

And finally, Christ-like love is costly. It requires us to walk by faith: that there is a God who sees the good we do and the injustices done to us, and who will deal with both on his own terms and in his own time. And, again, it's not about what we get out of it anyway. This love sacrifices itself. Christ-like love will be consistent and caring and will pay the cost for the needs of others. The cost will sometimes be our own happiness, our own reward and recognition, our own retribution and revenge, and maybe even our own life. Yes, certainly our own life one way or another. But it is not we who live anymore – it is Christ who lives in us (Gal. 2:20). This is the reason for this new command to love one another as Christ has loved us.

Christ-like love serves the dual purpose of embodying Christ to each other – making sure the family of God is cared for – but also embodying Christ to the world. Our love is consistent, caring, and costly because that is what has been modeled for us by Christ. No longer are we cutting our own hair off and tying granddaddy's shoelaces together – or much worse. We have given up the childish "gimme gimme gimme!" Christ wants to ensure that we have the best life he desires for us, and that we represent the best of the Father's family to the world. What Jesus says here of his own love is true in the lives of his followers: true love glorifies God, it allows God's light to shine in the darkest of situations and into the darkest of hearts. That is what it is for God's children to be on their best behavior. It isn't merely outward goodness that masks a darkened heart. We try that generation after generation and it always comes up empty. Not coincidentally we twist and strip the definition of love generation after generation and it always comes up empty.

But the new command of Christ-like love is the seed, the seed that dies to ideas of selfish glory for the sake of glorifying God in the act of love. For Jesus, to be on one's best behavior is very ugly, bloody business. Far from straightening your tie and sitting with your hands in your lap, Jesus' idea of best behavior is obeying everything he commands (Matt. 28:20). And the banner over all of it is LOVE. He says to "love one another as I have loved you." Then he takes up his cross and invites us to follow.

* * *

Friday. There he hangs, the bloody embodiment of divine glorification. His death is not just a seed; it is an example. Having turned the Temple on its head, he becomes the sacrifice. Once. For all. We look at the slain Lamb, at the collusion of human and satanic and natural evil, all gathered into the spotless one. He is the only one who can die this death. You can't do it for the world. You can't do it for yourself. This death is part of his calling. Even his desperately-doting heavenly Father can't do it for him. But while he is the only one who can die this death, he isn't the only one who dies. This is the way we must go as well. For Jesus, and for you and me, the path to glorious kingdom life leads through the cross, where this world's anemic and pathetic ideas of glory go to die. Now, Jesus says, at the cross, is the judgment of this world. Now, at the cross, is the satanic ruler of this world driven out. Now. At the cross. The lowest, darkest moment in human history is transformed into a note so bright that it rings and reverberates from creation's curse to kingdom come. At the cross.

And then the seed goes into the ground. Cold. Dark. Dead.

FOURTEEN

BEAT 3: GOD RISING

SUNDAY. SUNRISE. WOMEN, FOLLOWERS OF JESUS, come to his tomb to take care of his dead body (Mark 16:1; Luke 24:1). They are so sure that he is dead that their sole reason for going to the tomb is to prepare his body for burial. They aren't going to see if he's still there, checking on the body in the hopes that he might not really have died or has somehow come back to life. They are carrying spiced oil to embalm the body so it won't stink too much as it decays in death. They expect that the flesh will rot leaving only bones, which will be put into a box and removed to make room in the tomb for the next corpse. That's it. That's all. But there's a problem...

More about that in a minute but, first, a word about Christ's resurrection. We have to be careful that we don't make the mistake of thinking it's about proving that there's an afterlife, or even that we go to heaven when we die. That's not the point at all, really. We also have to be careful not to make another well-meaning mistake of thinking that Jesus' resurrection is about proving that he's divine. He is divine, but he wasn't raised *because* he's God. Again, this strips it of so much meaning.

So what is it about? If I had to put it in a sentence I would say the resurrection of Jesus the Son of God is about this: *Jesus' way is right.* He is who he said he is, and life is what he said it is. All that stuff about God's kingdom being among us, inside us, about heaven coming into the world, is right. The stuff about letting go of control is right. The stuff about God being with us, of God being in control, of life with God being true wealth and power, it's all right. The way of love, love and mercy and forgiveness even for enemies, is the right way. The stuff about Jesus being the one who is bringing God's kingdom reign into the world and into the lives of any- and everyone who longs for it...it's all so right you can stake your life on it. In fact, you *must* stake your life on it.

NAME

Early on the first day of the week, while it was still dark, Mary Magdalene went to the tomb and saw that the stone had been removed from the entrance.
- John 20:1

Do not fear, for I have redeemed you; I have called you by name; you are mine.
- Isaiah 43:1

Hi. I'm Robert. I'm Jamie's husband and Maddie Jane's father. I'm the son of Betty and Michael. I'm John's little brother. I am a pastor. I am a Texan. I am a writer and a musician. I like sports, especially baseball. I like to read, watch movies, listen to real vinyl records, and take road trips. I like Mexican food and blue is my favorite color.

So who are *you*? How do you answer that question? What is it people really want to know when they ask that? There are tons of people who want to know about you, usually so they can sell you something. Social networks, websites, corporations, stores, the government – all want to know who you are. Most folks don't want to get too deep, to know who we *really* are. But I'm asking. Are we our family? Are we our work? Are we our hobbies, interests, leisure activities? That's usually how we answer, the roles we play. But is that who we are? For millennia, philosophers, artists, scientists, writers, scholars of various sorts, and everyday people have sought the answer to the question. I suppose each of us spends most if not all of a lifetime trying to figure out who we are in the grand narrative of human history.

The people who hung around Jesus were no different. Even Jesus himself may have wondered who he really was at some point. If he did, he seemed to gain a pretty good understanding as his ministry progressed. And I would think by sunrise on Easter, there was no doubt whatsoever. There are several people mentioned in John's Easter story (Ch. 20), each one with something of an identifier: Jesus *the Lord* and *teacher*; Simon *the Rock* (the meaning of Simon's nickname, Peter); the disciple *whom Jesus loved*; God *the Father*; the angels who are literally God's *messengers*; a group probably of Jesus' disciples whom he refers to as his *brothers*.

And then there's Mary. She's the first one mentioned in John's Easter story, and she's called "the Magdalene" because she is from the town of Magdala. But that's just so she doesn't get confused with all the other Marys. That's not who she really is. There's a legend about her having been a prostitute, but that's not in the Bible. There's all that nonsense about her being Jesus' wife and the mother of his kids, but that's just trumped-up scandal to sell books of fiction. All we know is that Jesus cast seven demons out of Mary of Magdala and she became one of his closest and most faithful followers. Close and faithful follower…Ah! Now we're getting somewhere.

I think if we could ask this Mary who she is, this story might be her answer. "I'm Mary. The Lord saved me. I was with him right until his last breath. They took his body away and laid it in the tomb and I couldn't see it because it was the Sabbath. As soon as the Sabbath ended I was going to the tomb to finish preparing his body for burial. But when I got there, the stone was moved and his body was gone. I got scared and went to tell some others. They ran and looked in and, I didn't know what they saw, but they took off. I just stood there crying. I looked in and saw the Teacher's bandages and a couple of men in there, who asked me why I was crying. How could they ask such a thing! Then I turned around and saw who I thought was the gardener. He asked why I was crying and who I was looking for. I told him if he had taken my Lord's dead body away, to please tell me where it was so I could get it. Then he said my name...and then I knew."

The world has a lot of names for us: worker, family man, mom, consumer, success, addict, divorcee, failure, patient, 18-to-34, retiree, black, white, other, target audience, market-share, Boomer, X, Millennial, Republican, Democrat, Independent, winner, loser, picker, grinner, lover, sinner, and any number of identifiers our culture uses to try and make us fit. To most we're a demographic. But none of these things opens the door to who we really are. It's okay that some of these things *describe* us, but it's not okay when these things *define* us. Such tiny little labels can strip us of who God intends us to be, and can even strip us of the hope that we can ever really be anything. I wonder if Mary ever got to that point.

We don't know Mary's story, what these seven demons that Jesus cast out were driving her to do. Maybe she *was* a prostitute. Maybe she was an addict of some kind. Maybe she was abused and treated as property, never valued, cared for, or loved. Maybe she had given up on herself, given up on hope, and decided to do whatever it took to feel like she mattered – if only for a while.

And then Jesus comes. First, he makes her clean, gives her a fresh start. Then, he invites her into his life, to walk with him. She matters now, has a purpose. She's never seen a man treat a woman this way, especially not Mary-what's-her-name. She's part of a family. She's loved. You can imagine, then, how crushing it is when she stands there and watches him die. She is watching the death of a dear loved one. But she is also watching her own death and the death of any hope she has allowed into her heart. She still wants to hold on to Jesus –

even if it's just his lifeless body – just one more time before she opens the door to those demons again and goes back to being a filthy, discarded sinner. Because now, what's the use?

This is her plan when she goes to the tomb. This is her plan when she sees the stone rolled away. This is her plan when she goes and gets the others. This is her plan when she looks in for herself and sees the angels sitting there around the empty bandages. This is even her plan when she sort of half-sees Jesus and thinks he's the gardener. She just wants to know where they've taken the body so she can bury it and put it all to rest once and for all.

But then Jesus calls her by name. "Mary," he says. And hearing that word, she recognizes the risen Lord. And I think she recognizes herself for the first time. She is not Mary with the seven demons, or Mary the prostitute or the addict. She is not Mary what's-her-name or Mary from Magdala or just a sinner destined for death. She is Mary, the one Jesus calls by name. And because he is risen, he will forever call her by name. This is who she is. She begins to become.

Jesus tells her to go and tell the others that he is risen. She is the first one entrusted with the good news of Easter, that sin and death have been taken on by Jesus and defeated. She is the apostle ("sent one") to the apostles. And who better? Who better to announce the death of sin than one who had been so well acquainted with it? Who better to announce the resurrection of the Savior than one of the huddled few who stood with him to the very end? Now she gets to announce the new beginning! Who better than Mary, the one Jesus calls by name?

Jesus calls each of us by name. No matter where we've come from, what we've come through, or what others have called us, all that matters is that Jesus, the risen and very present Lord, calls you and me by name. No matter what kind of year you've had or what kind of life you've had, he calls you today, this second. God is present where you and I are

Beat 3: God Rising

right now, as I sit now and write and as you sit across time and space from me and read. He calls into the depths of our spirits, just as present where and when we are as he is in what we might consider the holiest of places or events or the vastness of the universe. Do we hear him and turn around and say, "Teacher! Lord!" Do we join him on the journey he's inviting us to? Or do we walk alone, clinging to the old, lifeless bodies of sin and death, peering into tombs for some bones of hope and purpose?

He is risen! It's the first day of forever. That moment of name-calling, when the risen Lord, the new Adam (1 Cor. 15:45) standing with a woman there in a garden on the first day of the eternal week, when he says Mary's name, it is the beginning of the new creation for her. Pause and picture that again: the new Adam and a woman, standing in a new garden, on the first day of a new week, speaking a new name. And as he says your name and mine, new creation begins in us. We welcome him and begin the process of becoming children of God. What does this mean? Answering that question is the journey. It begins today and it never ends.

I'm Robert – the one Jesus calls by name. Who are you?

ON THE ROAD

When he was at the table with them, he took bread, gave thanks, broke it and began to give it to them. Then their eyes were opened and they recognized him, and he disappeared from their sight. They asked each other, "Were not our hearts burning within us while he talked with us on the road...?"
- Luke 24:30-32

I love storytelling of most kinds, especially films. One of my favorite genres of storytelling is road stories and road movies. Some examples of road movies include *Little Miss Sunshine, Dumb & Dumber, Thelma & Louise, Rain Man, Stand By Me, Vacation,* and on back to *Easy Rider, Bonnie & Clyde,* the Bob Hope/Bing Crosby road pictures, *It Happened One Night,* and

The Wizard of Oz. You can probably think of other examples. One great one is *O Brother, Where Art Thou?* In addition to the fact that it's an epic Coen brothers film, it's also based on one of the oldest road stories, *The Odyssey*, which in its very title points to the fact that it's a road story.

I'd say there are three main characteristics that make a road story: 1) A personal crisis that sends the main character/s out; 2) Adventures on the road; and 3) Life lessons, and maybe a major revelation, that the character/s learn along the way that result in a deep change. There are lots of road stories in the Bible, including all four gospels. Of those, Luke is a master in his road Gospel and its sequel, Acts. And his Easter story (Luke 24) is a perfect example. So here is a loose treatment for a road movie we can call "Burning Hearts" – told in three parts, each with a vital question that comes to us and invites us into the story.

Part 1: The Crisis. Jesus is dead. His followers were sure he was going to overthrow Rome and become God's true anointed King of the Jews. But instead he was arrested, beaten, and executed – basically lynched for all to see. They took his dead body and laid it in a tomb two days ago. Now, Sunday morning, they are going to embalm the body and get it ready to be put away forever. But that's only the beginning of the crisis.

The women get to the tomb and…no body! They encounter what can only be supernatural beings – angels – and the angels ask one of the most brilliant questions ever asked: "Why do you look for the living among the dead?" The question is so brilliant that it echoes across the ages and comes to you and me right here and now: *Why do you look for the living among the dead?* What tombs do we haunt, looking for answers, for a life worth living? The dead past – relationships, wrongs, the good ol' days, abandoned dreams? How about the death the world dresses up to look alive – wealth, power, pleasure?

If we want to find Jesus – if we want the life that really is life (1 Tim. 6:19) – we have to leave the tombs behind. That's what his followers do that first Easter morning. They have their crisis of faith: What happened to Jesus and what does it all mean? So they hit the road to find out – to find God and maybe even to find themselves.

Part 2: The Adventure. A couple of Jesus' followers – a guy named Cleopas and his unnamed companion, probably his wife – leave Jerusalem and are heading home. They are talking with each other on the road about everything that has happened. As they're walking and talking, the risen Jesus sidles up next to them. Somehow they don't recognize him (something very different about his resurrection body seems to cause all of his friends not to recognize him at first). He asks what they're talking about as they walk along.

That's the next question that comes to you and me now as it came to that couple: *What are you talking about on your journey?* What story are we telling with our lives? Cleopas and his wife are talking about the same things we talk about: How things are (world problems); How things might've been (pipe dreams); How will it all work out (the unknown). We all have our versions of that life story, a life defined by problems and pipe dreams and grappling with the unknown future. For Cleopas and his wife in this moment it's Jesus' execution in Jerusalem (problems); their hopes that he might've been the Messiah (dreams); and the crisis of the missing body and the mysterious angelic encounter (unknown).

So they explain all this to Jesus, who has very humorously acted like he's totally unaware of any of it. He has acted like a clueless stranger and let them take the lead. But now he turns things around and starts teaching them from the scriptures, tying everything neatly together into the grand Jewish road story. They are all talking as they get near the end of their journey. Jesus acts like he's going to move on to the next town.

But it's late, so they invite him – this stranger – to come eat and stay with them.

Part 3: The Revelation. They are sitting together at the dinner table: Cleopas, his wife, and the unrecognized Jesus. They're eating and Jesus takes the bread, blesses it, breaks it, and gives it to them. And in that sacramental act of breaking the bread, Luke says, "Their eyes were opened and they recognized him." Jesus disappears and Cleopas and his wife are left sitting at the table. We're going to get to our third question, but first there's another quick story, a flashback.

There was another famous husband and wife whose eyes were opened when they were eating (Gen. 3). The big difference was, Adam and Eve were eating *apart from God*. When they ate the forbidden fruit, their eyes were opened and they saw their nakedness. They were ashamed and they hid from God. That began their journey on the road out of Eden, away from the fellowship with God they were made for. On the contrary, Cleopas and his wife are eating *with God*. They eat the bread Jesus gives them – the Bread of Life. Their eyes are opened and they see God. And this begins their journey on the road with God, the road home into God's kingdom.

The question they ask each other is: "Were not our hearts burning within us while he talked with us on the road?" They can only ask this, they can only look back and see how it all comes together, because their eyes are now open. They have fellowshipped with the risen Lord. And so that is our final question: *Are our hearts burning as we talk with him on the road?*

It comes down to the road. God is a Road God. That's what the entire next section of this book is about. It is vital to understand this about God…and about us. In Mark's Gospel, he doesn't even give us all these details and great resurrection stories (16:1-8). There possibly was another ending that is lost, and verses nine through twenty were added later. But in a providential way, Mark's short ending points perfectly to this active, living God. Mark gives sort of an X-Files ending, basically saying, "The Truth is out there. Jesus is risen and he's on the road...go find him!" But what would you expect from a risen Rock God – a cooped-up old man sitting in a rocking chair? No, he's on the road!

Following Jesus puts us at an interesting crossroads because it requires faith – belief that leads to action and life change – in two things: 1) There is a Jesus to follow (he's alive and active); and 2) Jesus invites us to come along (to share in his life and activity). For Cleopas and his wife the journey has just begun. Even though it's late and they're comfortable at home, they head out into the night to go back to Jerusalem and tell the others what happened. They are now people of the burning heart and they will never be the same – the world will never be the same.

And that's what it comes down to: Apart from Jesus, the world makes us; Following Jesus, we make the world. Are we on the road with the risen Jesus or are we still at the tomb? If we're at the tomb, as the angel said, "He is not here! He is risen!" If we're on the road with Jesus, our hearts will burn within us. We are living the life that is truly life. How do we live the burning heart? Leave the tombs behind, begin telling a new story, and hit the road. The journey of the burning heart is just beginning.

FIFTEEN

BEAT 4: GOD MAKING ALL THINGS NEW

SO JESUS IS OUT THERE, on the road. This isn't just the result of his resurrection, though. There's another big moment that we Christians often overlook. Jesus gathers his followers on the hill one last time (Acts 1:1-11). They are all caught up in what will happen next, asking him if now is the time that he'll get back on the worldly track of kingdom-building. The answer is yes, Jesus is about kingdom-building. But it isn't what they think, and they needn't get caught up in time-frames. "You will receive power when the Holy Spirit comes on you," Jesus assures them. "And you will be my witnesses locally, regionally, globally." Power with a purpose.

Like Mr. Miyagi taught Daniel in *The Karate Kid* with the whole "wax on, wax off" bit, there comes a time when our training must come alive. We do drills in sports, learn scales in music, practice our lines, learn our steps – we study and learn and practice, practice, practice. But at some point we have to get in the game, start jamming, play the part, dance the dance, take the test, graduate, and grow up.

The Ascension and Pentecost are about graduating to a whole new way of being God's people under the reign of

Christ the King. Jesus steps into heaven, leaving the bewildered disciples with their mouths hanging open. "Why do you stand here looking into the sky?" the angels ask. Jesus has gone into heaven, and he'll come back. But you have work to do on earth. The fact that Jesus has ascended means he is in the place of authority at "the right hand of God" (Luke 22:69). The King of heaven and earth is on his throne. This authority is exercised on earth in large part through his church, and through his eventual return to bring God's kingdom into fullness in his creation – the new heavens and new earth (Is. 65:17; Rev. 21:1). But now is indeed the time that the kingdom is coming. And something else is coming too: the power.

HEARING THE MUSIC

> *...this is what was spoken by the prophet Joel: "In the last days, God says, I will pour out my Spirit on all people. Your sons and daughters will prophesy, your young men will see visions, your old men will dream dreams. Even on my servants, both men and women, I will pour out my Spirit in those days, and they will prophesy...And everyone who calls on the name of the Lord will be saved."*
> - Acts 2:16-18, 21

Imagine you've never really heard music. You know there's this wonderful thing called music. And you've kind of heard it. Once a year, you take your family to the city, and one representative of all the people goes into a concert hall and listens to invisible, mystery musicians playing, say, Mozart's Requiem Mass – choirs and strings and horns and the most achingly powerful music ever created. Or, if you like, a rock concert featuring epics like "Bohemian Rhapsody," "You Can't Always Get What You Want," "Comfortably Numb," "Hotel California," "2112," "Silent Lucidity," "November Rain," and on and on, closing with "Kashmir" and "A Day in the Life." Boom!

Then, that representative comes out of the concert hall and proceeds to try and sing what he's just heard. Oh, he does a fine job; after all, he's the best singer of all the people. And you don't really know what you're missing, so it sounds ok to you. But then, one magnificent day, you and all in your community who have been hungering to hear the song again, your heads fill with music. You're hearing harmony where you had only known melody, strings and horns where you had only known a voice, rhythm and percussion where there had only been syllables. Not only are people hearing this in their heads, they begin to fashion instruments to replicate the sounds from their heads. They join together and start playing music, and some even begin dancing! No longer do you just know *about* the music. Now you're *in* the music, and the music is in you. The possibilities seem endless, and life becomes art.

Pentecost is the day when God's people really began to hear the music. I believe we drastically undervalue Pentecost and its ramifications. In the first creation "week," God made humans and breathed his breath of life into them (Gen. 2:7). As Christ's resurrection "on the first day of the week" was the beginning of the new creation, so Pentecost is the moment when God breathes life – Spirit life (a number of languages, including Hebrew and Greek, utilize one word for "spirit," "wind," and "breath") – into all who would be born again. Kind of important. And, when understood as the fulfillment of centuries of prophetic hope, Pentecost should be celebrated with Christmas and Easter as another divine proclamation of the God who is Immanuel, "God with us."

Pentecost is the fulfillment and renewal of the Law. The Jewish feast of Pentecost, fifty days after Passover, was the feast that marked the giving of the Law. Death had passed over the Hebrew first-born, while destroying the first-born of their oppressors, finally convincing Pharaoh to set Israel free from slavery. Fifty days after leading his people safely through the Red Sea, Moses was given the Law, among God's wind and fire on Mt. Sinai. The people rode a roller coaster of obedience and disobedience to this law for more than a millennium until that miraculous Pentecost moment when God's Spirit began to write the Law on tablets of flesh, the very lives of God's people. Now, the Law of the Spirit is written on human hearts, enabling us to live lives that worship God in spirit and in truth (John 4:24).

Pentecost is the fulfillment and renewal of the Temple. This stuff of wind and fire is descriptive of God's presence in the Old Testament, from the pillars of cloud and fire that Moses and the people followed through the wilderness to the fiery experience of God's heavenly temple that the prophets Isaiah and Ezekiel both had. By the first century AD, many Jews were awaiting fulfillment of the prophecy that the Lord would return to his Temple and fill it with his glory and power. Of course, part of that return happened when Jesus visited the Temple in judgment (see, for example, Mark 11:12-26). But really, this is it. The big twist is that the Lord did return to fill his temple, but the temple turns out not to be one built with human hands, but God's own handiwork – the Church universal, the Body of which Christ himself is the Head. The temple of God is the lives of believers, individually, but especially collectively as the church. And we show God's power and glory in the gifts and fruit – the life – of the Spirit. And the banner over it all is "Love."

One other prophecy was fulfilled that Pentecost day, and continues to this one: When the Lord returned to fill his temple, the nations would flock to the holy city to hear the word of the Lord (Mic. 4:2). And so it is as Luke reports it – representatives from all sorts of scattered nations stand in awe as they hear the transformational word of God proclaimed in their own tongue. The nations hunger for the good news of new life in Christ and God's kingdom come. And just as Jesus promised only ten days before all this, his followers receive power when the Holy Spirit fills them – power to proclaim the good news and witness to Christ's saving love.

Do we hear the music? Do we dare to dance? For the Jews, to read or hear the Law was to encounter the presence of God – to look into his heart – and the Temple was the place where God's glory was revealed and he was rightly worshipped. The Law and the Temple were places where heaven and earth overlapped. Now, each and all of us are that place – the place where God is worshipped in spirit and truth; the place where God's power and glory are displayed; and the place where God's reconciliation in Christ is proclaimed to all the world. This should affect the way we read Scripture, the way we worship and view the church, the way we understand the ministry of all believers – in short, the way we live our born-again lives. So pick up an instrument and play your part. Get in the circle and join the dance. But dance with bare feet, for everywhere you stand is holy ground.

THE CENTER OF THE UNIVERSE

Now to him who is able to do immeasurably more than all we ask or imagine, according to his power that is at work within us, to him be glory in the church and in Christ Jesus throughout all generations, for ever and ever! Amen.
- Ephesians 3:20-21

My calling to pastoral ministry was a little odd. Other pastors talk about growing up in church, about how much it meant to them. They remember little old ladies pinching their cheeks and telling them they will make a fine pastor some day. They tell of youth pastors and mentor pastors giving them leadership roles and letting them try on pastoring for size. There seems to be a rather clearly marked path that led right through college to seminary and into the pulpit.

Not me. True, I was a child in church. I have memories of Pastor Ken Metzger yelling passionate sermons (and even scaring me a little), of Pastor Buff Hearn playing his guitar in

Beat 4: God Making All Things New

church (can you really do that?), of my mom playing the organ, of going to Sunday school and Vacation Bible School. And of course, my chubby cheeks were sufficiently pinched. I was a well-behaved church kid. But I didn't stay very active in church. And I was certainly never going to become a pastor.

In high school, during homecoming week, we had those crazy dress-up days. You know, everyone's supposed to dress like a nerd or a slob or wear pajamas (for some, of course, these were just everyday outfits). One of the dress-up days was career day, where you were supposed to dress in the garb of the career you hoped to go into. My friend Thomas McKenzie dressed in black with a priest's clerical collar. I wore ripped jeans and spandex (don't judge – it was the 80s), extra-long earrings, and a cut-up shirt with Mozart on it. Today, Thomas is a fine Anglican priest. I, on the other hand, missed the mark a bit with my rock star wardrobe.

Things changed. After several years as a musician, there were a number of steps along the road that eventually did lead me on to seminary and into the pastorate. But there was one main thing that opened my eyes and heart to this calling: I fell in love with the church.

It wasn't just memories of bazaars and revivals and Christmas Eve candlelight services; of my grandfather being the first to arrive at church on Sunday to turn on the lights and make the coffee, and my grandmother leading Bible studies for the ladies' circles. It was those things. But more than that, it was mind-blowing stuff like this:

> *I ask the God of our Master, Jesus Christ, the God of glory, to make you intelligent and discerning in knowing him personally, your eyes focused and clear, so that you can see exactly what it is he is calling you to do, grasp the immensity of this glorious way of life he has for his followers, oh, the utter extravagance of his work in us who trust him – endless energy, boundless strength!*

> *All this energy issues from Christ: God raised him from death and set him on a throne in deep heaven, in charge of running the universe, everything from galaxies to governments, no name and no power exempt from his rule. And not just for the time being, but forever. He is in charge of it all, has the final word on everything. At the center of all this, Christ rules the church. The church, you see, is not peripheral to the world; the world is peripheral to the church. The church is Christ's body, in which he speaks and acts, by which he fills everything with his presence.* (Eph. 1:17-23)[12]

Not a bad way to spend a life. Of course one needn't be a pastor to be part of this. (Indeed, that might be a last resort for many of us.) No, it's the people: organ-playing moms and coffee-making grandfathers, guitar-playing pastors and cheek-pinching old ladies, young and old women and men with light or dark skin in cathedrals or tin-roofed shacks playing organs or djembes, thousands in an arena or a dozen in a living room – all knit together...forever...joined to God at the center of eternity. Even you and me.

Sadly, we think we have it all figured out. Turn on your TV to any so-called "news" channel and you will see it: politicians stumbling over themselves to grab the power and authority of the White House; trusted coaches and even religious leaders who pervert and abuse their power and authority; celebrities who set trends and make obscene amounts of money, often just for being famous, and who don't seem to answer to authority the same way the rest of us do; and on and on... people grabbing for money, sex, and power. And not one of them having any idea what real power is.

But perhaps saddest of all is the fact that so many Christians fall right in line with them, buying the lie that real life is experienced through having more money, more pleasure, more approval and adulation. Now certainly we are no better than those who cling to the things of this world for meaning – we are all subject to the same temptations. But we have no excuse for continuing to stumble with the same near-sightedness. Here's what I mean.

If I take off my glasses or contacts, everything becomes a blur. I can see what's right in front of my face but, beyond just a few feet out, everything becomes a mass of color and edgeless shapes. I certainly can't see the details that make up the bigger picture. This is all fine if I just live according to what's right in front of me, according to my own little vision of things. But what happens if someone gives me glasses? Wow! When did all this get here?

I invite you to forget everything you think you know about power and pleasure and the meaning of life, to move all the power-hungry and fame-hungry and money-hungry people to the side, and to accept this pair of glasses: "At the center of all this, Christ rules the church. The church, you see, is not peripheral to the world; the world is peripheral to the church. The church is Christ's body, in which he speaks and acts, by which he fills everything with his presence."

No one, no matter how rich or powerful or famous in the world's eyes, has the power to free the world from sin and death, rise from the dead, and sit at the right hand of God – the place of true authority – and to rule the universe. That's Jesus Christ...only Jesus Christ. But let me tell you a secret... lean in close for this one: He shares that power with you and me. Those who turn their lives over to Jesus Christ are set free and will rise from the dead and will reign with him. If you have given him your sin and your death and your life, then that life is hidden with him at the center of the universe, the center of everything. Not that you or I are the center of everything. But he is, and you can be one with him.

The world's powers don't have that authority – not over the universe and not over you. You don't have to play by their rules. You and I aren't really the center, but they're certainly not the center of it all, either. Money, pleasure, and power. Climbing ladders and numbing pain and puffing up. All for what? Jesus is shaking everything and, in the end, only the unshakable will remain (Heb. 12:27). Your life in Christ is unshakable. It's a done deal, no matter how things seem. Let all that other stuff go. Put your glasses on and see how amazing it all really is, and give him thanks. Thank him for his beautiful creation and for your beautiful life…and for his beautiful church, through whom he is filling all the world with his power, his presence, and his love.

PART IV:
ROAD

What a long, strange trip it's been...
- The Grateful Dead

SIXTEEN

ROAD GOD

BACK IN MY DAYS TRYING to make a living as a musician I had mixed feelings about life on the road, enjoying the freedom of wandering but also longing for home. This paradox is shared by most troubadours, reflected in songs like Grand Funk's "We're an American Band" and The Rolling Stones' "Torn and Frayed" and Willie Nelson's "On the Road Again," as well as Journey's "Faithfully" and Mötley Crüe's "Home Sweet Home" and Bon Jovi's "Wanted Dead or Alive" and Simon and Garfunkel's "Homeward Bound." Most musicians have something in their catalog about both sentiments, heading out and coming home. This is road life.

From coffee houses and dive bars to larger clubs and concert halls on up to coliseums and stadiums, if a band wants to make it they have to get the music to the people. The road is often a proving ground. If you can't play it live, then you probably don't have any business in the business. Especially in this age of cell-phone video and YouTube, being bad on the road can ruin a career. But the road is also what can make a good musician better. It's where the music is strengthened night after night, and where that joy in the journey and longing for home come together to make new songs. But it's also where musicians who don't know what they're really about can lose themselves to detachment and debauchery. To succeed on the road you have to know your music, know your message, know yourself.

One time I was driving from California to Texas. I was a young wanderer living that "Bobby McGee" kind of freedom – you know, nothing left to lose. I was alone and very sleep-deprived, zoning out for miles at a time. I had made the drive so many times that I could do it with my eyes closed, and I think I tried a couple of times. This time, however, I ran into a bit of a snag. There in the middle of the desert, at a crossroads with a gas station, a diner, and a stop light, I faced a sign that read "Road Closed: Detour." *No biggie,* I thought, *I'll be back on track in a few miles*. Famous last thoughts…

Miles and miles went by and I never saw another detour sign to get me back on my intended journey. Before long I saw signs for towns that I'd never heard of, or that I knew were nowhere near the direction I needed to be going. And they weren't coming up soon – we're talking a couple hundred miles. I'd heard of the middle of nowhere and now apparently I'd found it. I was whizzing past desert scrub – a cactus here, a Joshua tree there, the occasional scraggly palm, sage hills around me and endless blacktop in front of me. It was a never-ending two-lane highway through the Twilight Zone. Now it was twenty minutes since I detoured…now thirty minutes… now forty-five. I abandoned all hope that I would ever see another detour sign. But I kept thinking surely I would come to a town where I could get directions and get back on track.

Suddenly my stomach sank as I realized I hadn't checked my gas gauge in a while. I actually thought about it before looking at it, as if not knowing how much gas I had (or didn't have) might be better – at least I wouldn't start worrying about that too. But I looked and, sure enough, there was my little needle rubbing flirtatiously up against the red zone. And there I was, in the middle of nowhere, running out of gas and heading for Mexico.

* * *

There are two crucial understandings in such a situation. First, one must understand what it is to be lost. Second, one must understand what it is to be found. This is, in a very broad sweep, the biblical story and the life of faith. The fallen world is notorious for evading that first issue, continuing to willfully careen down a highway to hell, away from God, even sometimes calling it "the good life." But the people of God are notorious for evading the second issue, continuing to sit on our hands in our holy huddle, choking on a list of superficial do's and don'ts and calling it "holiness."

What are we supposed to be doing? Why don't we just step into heaven after we "get saved"? And is that what Christianity is about, getting into heaven when we die? Or is being a Christian about doing good deeds? What is holiness, anyway? We have planted all sorts of detour signs along the road in response to these questions: Legalism; Liberalism; Liberation; Left Behind; Evangelicalism; Enthusiasm; Tolerance; Turn-or-Burn; Calvinism; Arminianism; Christian hedonism; Desert asceticism; Apocalypse Now; Apocalypse Never; One Way; Many Ways; I'll Fly Away, O Glory! Take your pick. God is big, his plans are big, and it is never safe to claim a monopoly on the truth. Nevertheless, it seems clear that many today have a limited-to-non-existent awareness that something really happened upon Jesus' resurrection, something more than proving that there is life after death and showing how to get to heaven when we die. It's as if he was about getting us into heaven – or heaven into us, really – *before* we die. And when the fiery light of Pentecost is thrown on it all, the people of God becoming the temple of God, things get extra-interesting. It was a whole new thing. For the wanderers who will turn onto that road it becomes a whole new creation; indeed, *they* become a whole new creation.

God is a Road God. Not a road god like Willie Nelson or Jerry Garcia, but a big-"G" God who reveals himself and his kingdom on the road. He's out there. Yes, he's in here. But he's also out there. We are made for this world. Maybe we're not made for it as it is – as we've made it, really. In that "fallen" sense we and the world are perfect for each other. But no, "The creation waits in eager expectation for the children of God to be revealed" (Rom. 8:19). From the beginning, this was our special place, the place for us to live and thrive and cultivate and nurture and bear fruit, all under the loving lordship of our Creator-Father who called it all "very good." This plan was not scrapped, despite our best efforts to thwart it all. In the end it is all made new, but never scrapped.

Things changed that first Easter. They continued to change that first Pentecost. You can't stop the change, can't hope to contain it. But it's happening and it's sweeping us along with it. We're not heading for the clouds or for a spirit world. Ultimately we're not even heading for heaven, at least not some far-off heaven the way we usually think of it. But we're also not heading back to the garden. We're heading for something completely new, the likes of which we can't comprehend. But the only way to get there is to hit the road following the Road God. Because as any good rocker knows, even in this internet age, the best way to build an audience and to spread the music and the message is still the old-fashioned way: takin' it to the streets.

Maybe we don't realize that the new creation started on that first Easter morning. Maybe we don't want to realize it. Maybe right now is the first you've heard of it, and maybe later you'll wish you hadn't. Living in the present reality of the new creation means we don't get to just shake our heads at those poor, lost sinners while we hide together and sing songs about flying away from it all. And living in the new creation means we don't get to turn the church into a club of do-gooders without any real change within ourselves. No, if the new creation has begun – or more, if we're two thousand years into it – then we're on the hook. Things should be different, starting with us.

* * *

Clueless and gasless and heading for Mexico, I finally decided I would take the next road that went east. *"Texas is a big place,"* I thought, *"and even though I don't know where I am, if I just start heading east maybe I'll get there eventually."* I turned onto a small, cracked highway and made it up into the distant hills and basically coasted down, and there I happened upon a little town. In my troubled mind it was salvation, like Bethlehem housing the hope of my mobile world. I rolled into the quickie mart on fumes, filled up, bought a map, and got myself back on track and eventually back to Texas.

It's time to turn east (so to speak). Life is too short and narrow not to step into something beyond our little circumstances. And the world is too small and fractured not to carry it with us into that something beyond. Don't we want to leave a legacy of holiness for the next generations beyond just *do* dress nice for Sunday school and *don't* curse or chew or go with girls that do; *do* support the right political party and *don't* have a beer in your fridge or cable on your TV; *do* love the sinner but hate the sin and *don't* associate with the wrong sorts of people; or whatever little holy lists we make up? Don't we want to be the kind of people through whom God's kingdom is coming on earth as it is in heaven? In short, don't we want to be spittin'-image, chip-off-the-ol'-block offspring of the Rock God? If so, then it starts right here, right now, spilling out from inside each of us – struggling wanderers filled with the power of perfect love, the power to become children of God. Stumbling or running, we find ourselves on a road.

SEVENTEEN

WANDERERS

HANGING IN MY STUDY IS a painting done in 1818 by the German Romantic painter, Caspar David Friedrich, called "The Wanderer Above the Sea of Fog." The print was given to me by a dear friend and mentor, the first person to invite me into leadership and ministry, who said it made him think of me. It means a lot to me and it has spoken to me on different levels and at various times in my life.

There are several things going on in this painting. The wanderer stands on top of a rocky precipice he has just scaled. He looks out over a layer of fog that stretches out of sight and becomes one with the horizon and the sky. Jutting up from the fog are a few other ridges, and then a higher peak in the distance. It's a relatively simple picture, very balanced compositionally, but not particularly radical or attention grabbing. It's a quiet picture, and strong.

That's what draws me to it – its quiet strength. There are three specific things that most bind me to the picture. First, the sea of fog: It is the unknown, covering everything in mystery, and it seems to go on forever. Second, the wanderer: He isn't collapsed from exhaustion or looking back at what he has just accomplished. Instead, he's standing tall and looking ahead to future journeys. Third, the distant mountain: The wanderer has just scaled a pretty serious height, but he's looking at even higher mountains that still need to be climbed. For me, this picture is about life on the road of faith: the inward strengthening of faith, the onward journey of faith, and the upward goal of faith.

I always live this picture in its symbolic sense, but I also lived it in its literal sense one time. I was living in California's Sierra Nevada Mountains. Every day, I would drive past a number of hilly peaks on my forty-five minute descent to work 5,000 feet below. There was one peak – not too high, but not too low – that I always told myself I would climb. One day I finally set out to do it. I parked my car at the base and started up with a little backpack with water and my Bible. I climbed and rested, climbed and rested, thinking a number of times that I'd gone far enough. The hill was higher than it had looked from the bottom (aren't they always). But what drove me on was a burning necessity to know what was on the other side. There were a couple of mountain resort towns in the area, so I began to imagine what the cabins and houses and pristine golf courses would look like from my lofty perch. I dropped the backpack after a while and left it behind, tucking my small Bible into my waistband. I took off my shirt and tied it around my waist. Sweat trickled down my back and dripped from my nose, but I was determined. I had to reach the top. I had to know what was on the other side. As I neared what I desperately hoped was the summit the sky darkened and the wind intensified. Finally, I made it. I looked behind me, across the glorious valley and other peaks I'd left behind. I eagerly walked across the summit to look at the other side. And there I saw it: another mountain.

Despite my twinge of disappointment, I went on to have a powerful time of prayer in that spot, a very personal discussion with God that has continued over the years to be deeply meaningful. But it wasn't until I had carried on, returned home, and awoken the next day to see the "Wanderer" painting that I realized that he, too, was looking at another, higher peak ahead of him.

I was thinking recently that this could be a picture of the apostle Thomas after his encounter with the risen Jesus (John 20:24-29) and, as such, a general picture of the life of faith. Thomas walks around for a week doubting the reports of his brothers- and sisters-in-the-faith that Jesus is risen from the dead. Then, when Jesus comes again to them, he singles Thomas out and invites him to touch his wounds. We don't know if Thomas actually touches them – John doesn't say. One would think seeing the risen Lord standing there was enough. Whatever the case, he does end up believing. But then Jesus seems to rebuke "doubting" Thomas, saying, "You believe because you've seen me. Blessed are those who have not seen and yet believe."

So, for Thomas, the crucifixion and the reports of the resurrection were like a sea of fog, forcing him to look inward at his doubts and fears. Imagine what that week after the crucifixion and resurrection would've been like for Thomas, the sorrow and longing confused by the whispers of hope and rumors of glory. Then, seeing the risen Lord sets him on a lofty peak where he can see the big picture. The new creation has begun. Jesus really is a King and Conqueror above and beyond any before. But Jesus' rebuke sets Thomas's eyes on the higher peaks ahead. The church will be persecuted and scattered. Thomas will take the gospel all the way to India, the only apostle to carry the good news beyond the Roman Empire. There, Thomas will be killed for his faith. But suffering and even death are only a farther ascent, upward toward a higher union with the Father. Thomas will go inward, onward, and upward, because he is a new creature.

* * *

This can easily be a picture of any of us. We all wander and encounter seas of fog and face daunting peaks, even (perhaps especially) on the road in the new creation. We struggle to make sense of it all, hoping the day will come when we no longer wander and the fog dissipates and there are no more mountains to climb and everything is nice and easy. But what kind of life is that, really? Maybe we're looking at it all wrong. If we have entrusted our lives to the risen Christ, we have been born again, born from above – God has breathed the life of new creation into us. Now this should mean that we have set out on the journey, becoming part of the new creation. The foggy range need no longer be a strange and frightening place.

We should be diligently cultivating the *inward* life of faith. Through prayer, worship, fasting, study, solitude, and other ways of training our minds, hearts, souls, and strength, we overcome the fear of the unknown and learn to discern and trust the Lord's leading, even if we can't see him. We learn to love Love and to follow Love's lead.

We should be walking the *onward* journey of faith. If we dedicate ourselves to living as Christ's disciples – loving others, making right choices, looking for new opportunities to give and to serve, letting go the kingdoms of this world to hold tightly to the grace of God – then we see the very towers of God's kingdom rising around us.

And we should be seeking the *upward* goal of faith. If we seek God in every situation and every moment of our lives, removing obstacles to intimacy and experiencing nothing less than the life of the Trinity, then even the greatest obstacles in our lives are only things that lift us closer to God – even death itself.

Unfortunately, there are many variations on this painting in our lives. Sometimes we are wanderers *drowning in* the sea of fog. We are so afraid of the unknown that we just curl up and sit in the mist. We let our fear kill our inward faith, unwilling to believe that God is lovingly and powerfully taking care of things. Then we are the wanderers *asleep on* the sea of fog. Our focus is backward, not onward. We are either so proud of, or so beaten up by, the past that we have no interest in going forward. And sometimes we are wanderers *oblivious to* the sea of fog. We are so heavenly minded that we're no earthly good.

We just look at where the fog disappears into the sky and imagine the day when we'll fly away into that sky. In the mean time we turn a blind eye to all those poor wretches down there in the fog.

But the new creature, living in the new creation, should have their sights inward, onward, and upward. We have the chance to be those "blessed" ones Jesus spoke of to Thomas, those ones who have not seen yet still believe. We study and pray and worship and learn to trust God so we can keep following him, even in the fog. We dedicate ourselves to loving and serving others, no matter how much good or bad we've already done or how much has been done to us. And we stop building our own little kingdom and we enter into the intimate joy of being co-creators with God, working for his kingdom and glory on earth. What a thrilling and terrifying journey it all is – but only if we'll hit the road. The new creation has started. Those in Christ are new creatures, living new lives and co-creating a new world (2 Cor. 5:16-21). The old has gone, the new has come. I can't say it any better than what Jesus told Thomas so simply: "Stop doubting. Start believing."

EIGHTEEN

THE CYCLE OF BECOMING

WHO DOESN'T LOVE A GOOD DEMONSTRATION? I was raised, even as a child, going to "No Nukes" rallies and concerts for peace. But my years serving among the church have changed my youthful belief that if we just get out and end poverty and hunger and disease and war, then the world will become God's kingdom. And I left behind the youthful period of navel-gazing, believing that the goal of all things is to flee earthly troubles by getting in touch with some spirit world. And I also left behind the pastoral goals of simply getting warm bodies seated comfortably in pews and building a strong organization. I left all this behind for the power to become a child of God.

Perhaps the most magnificent promise in human history is that those who receive Christ are given the power to become children of God, new creations born of God's will and God's power (John 1:12-13). This becoming, the work of God's grace alone, is nonetheless a cyclical process. The cycle of becoming begins with our standing before God, moves to our standing before our neighbors, and ends with our standing before God. Jesus described it as being part of the flow of real life, that those who thirst for real life should come to him and drink. Then they would be filled with the streams of living water (John 7:38). These streams flow from within, but they are supposed to flow from believers out to the world. And then they must carry the world back to Jesus, because he is the

Source. He is the one inviting the thirsty to come to him and drink. So the thirsty come to Jesus, they are filled and poured out to others who are thirsty, they lead the others to the Source, from whom they are filled in order to be poured out, and the cycle continues every moment of every day until "the earth is filled with the knowledge of the Lord as the waters cover the sea" (Is. 11:9).

What does this look like? I'll tell you what it doesn't look like: headlines. I remember sitting at the dinner table with my wife and our then six-month-old daughter, reflecting on the news – war, corruption, starvation, scandal, disease, greed, etc., etc., etc. You know what I'm talking about. I was sickened in my depths at the thought of my child growing up amidst such horror. And I was just as sickened wondering what her generation might do with such a majestic mess. *"She's so innocent,"* I sat there thinking. *"Where is the change? Where are the heroes? Who's going to fix everything?"* But I couldn't get away from the fact that I must do more than just change the community or change the government or change the world. I have to start changing myself – Gandhi's "be the change you want to see in the world" and all that. Then I realized I couldn't just raise my daughter as a good human being. I had to raise her as a sister in Christ with the power to become a child of God – a human becoming.

Yes, those answers I once looked to are important. Ending poverty and hunger and disease and war is a good thing, and part of the church's call. Self-examination and spirituality are good things and part of the church's call. And belonging to a community of faith and worshiping together are good things and key aspects of the church's call. But such disparate paths – in and of themselves – wind up in the same place, the place of having the "form of godliness but denying its power" (2 Tim. 3:5). It is as if the living water is actually a stream of vodka – it has the appearance of water, but the results of drinking from that stream are drastically different. So activism or spirituality or even church life for their own sakes are self-centered and, ultimately, more destructive than creative. They do accomplish some good, but they can also become idols serving as substitute gods. For, ultimately, the change we want to see in the world is not just good, but God.

In the end, it is a matter of lived values. You are a human being, but you are also a human becoming – you are a person in process, whether you are intentional about it or not. If you are a new creature in the new creation, you have the power to become a child of God and, therefore, should be becoming more like Jesus Christ, the Son of God. This means that you play certain riffs – faith and justice and peace and care and beauty. You play a certain rhythmic story – God coming and God dying and God rising and God making all things new. You live certain values which reflect the heart and mind of the Father. And these values cannot be merely outward or merely inward.

As we become, so we act. As we act, so we become. But we must first be intentional about our becoming, and about the lived values that guide our becoming. We must become like the King if we are to know and do his will and be agents of his kingdom. And, as we live more intentionally and deeply into the kingdom, the more like the King we become. Otherwise we are building our own kingdoms – whether of (self-)righteousness like activism and spirituality and church empires, or of greed or consumption or pleasure or even family and relational networks – and they will only be reflections of us, and they will die as surely as we will. But for those who are becoming children of God, what we are becoming goes on just as surely as our Father goes on...forever and in power. And so, ultimately, as God's reign advances in our lives, it is God himself advancing across the world.

As a Beatles fan and a spiritually oriented person, I've always been a fan of George Harrison's stuff. I know his spiritual quest took him on a different path from my own. But

The Cycle of Becoming

I appreciate that he seemed to be making a disciplined attempt, which was reflected in the lyrics of the songs he wrote. Now I'm a big fan of Lennon's "All You Need is Love" – the song and the concept. But for me "Here Comes the Sun" is much deeper and subtler. It's a promise for all the wanderers. In the name of redemption I'm lifting it up as a pilgrim song, a kingdom song. This is especially appropriate in light of the glorious prophetic promise that concludes the Old Testament: "But for you who revere my name, the sun of righteousness will rise with healing in its wings" (Mal. 4:2). As Easter people our Easter lives are about showing the good news, echoing from that first Easter sunrise: the winter has been long and cold and lonely...but here comes the sun!

NINETEEN

THE NEW WORLD

EVER HAVE A LIFE-CHANGING EXPERIENCE – or even just something really significant – and then try to go back to life as you knew it before? There are things like graduation, your wedding, the birth of a child. Sometimes it's a more random event. But you're different...the world seems different. And life just can't be the same.

Another fruitless night. Peter and the gang have gotten back to life-as-they-knew-it: fishing (John 21). But it's just not the same. You can imagine the quietness on the boat, the night filled with unspoken questions. What are we doing? What are we supposed to be doing? Did we really see Jesus? What can it all mean? And for Christ-denying Peter, What have I done? Can it ever be the same again?

Sunrise. Jesus stands on the shore, watching them about a hundred yards out. He rather sarcastically calls to them, "Hey, friends! Catch anything?" Thinking he's just some obnoxious stranger they grunt back, "No." "Try the other side of the boat," Jesus says. Desperate to make something of their long night, they give it a shot and the net is so full they can't get it onto the boat. In that moment they know it's Jesus.

Peter jumps in the water and swims to shore while the others tow the catch back in. When they get up on the beach they find Jesus sitting next to a campfire. Peter sits down and warms his hands. The last time we saw Peter warming himself by a fire, he was denying he even knew Jesus. It seems John wants us to remember that – that part of the story isn't over yet. But first, it's time to eat. Jesus already has some fish and bread cooking on his fire. He invites them to bring some of the fish they've caught.

I think right there we have a picture coming together of life in the New World. They try to return to life-as-they-knew-it, but it just wasn't the same. Jesus invites them to try things differently and they find fruitfulness and satisfaction. They join Jesus in a sort of everyday fellowship, eating together on the beach. He doesn't *need* their fish, but he invites them to bring what they have into what he's doing. He *could* do it alone, but he chooses not to – he wants to live and work with his people, for his people to live and work with him. But what's driving the whole thing? Is it just Jesus' desire for them to fish for people, to save the world? That *is* it, but there's something deeper.

Jesus calls Peter aside. The fresh morning air is thick with tension. "Do you love me?" Jesus asks. "Yes, Lord," is the answer, "you know that I love you." They have this exchange three times, one for each of Peter's denials. But is it that simple – just a sentimental exchange? Certainly the words "I love you" are powerful. But Jesus adds something, something life-changing...world-changing. "Take care of my sheep," Jesus replies each time.

Two important things are happening here. First, Jesus' forgiveness includes action, trust, an invitation. Jesus doesn't *say*, "Ok, I forgive you." Instead, the Good Shepherd invites the forgiven one to live and work with him – much more powerful. And second, this means that our life spent with Jesus is driven, not just by a desire to get people saved or even to change the world. Our life with Jesus is driven by love for him. "I love you, Lord." "Ok, then come do what I'm doing." Love comes first.

There's a lot of mystery here. It's perfect that it happens at dawn, that kind of hazy, color-filled time after a long, hard night. There's a miraculous catch of fish just by Jesus commanding it...strange. They sit with Jesus on the beach, but John adds this very weird line: "None of them dared ask him, 'Who are you?' They knew it was the Lord." Why does John, who never wastes a word, need to tell us that? Like Mary outside the tomb and Cleopas and his companion on the Emmaus Road, the disciples here don't instantly recognize him. The Gospel writers don't tell us what the risen Jesus was like, but there's something very different about him. It's all a very different, even strange time. Yet it's also a very ordinary day of work and breakfast with friends and patching up a strained relationship.

This is the New World: the miraculous in the everyday, living and working with the risen Lord of heaven and earth, loving him and sharing his love for the church – his sheep – and for the world. And it all starts with two magic words. You want magic in your life? You want a miracle? Then here are the two magic words that Jesus said to Peter, he has said in one mysterious way or another to each human for two thousand years, and he says to you and me right now: "Follow me." Every day, in your work, your relationships, your thoughts and plans, Jesus extends the same invitation to each and all of us: "Follow me." Not partway, not just sometimes; all of you – the real you – all the time, on the road into the mysterious sunrise of the New World. Follow me.

PART V:
ROOTS

A singer becomes a soul singer when he decides to reveal rather than conceal. When he takes what's on the inside and brings it to the outside.
- Bono

TWENTY

ROCK GOD

I WAS IN THE CEREAL AISLE when I heard it. *"It's The Ramones,"* I thought. *"I Wanna Be Sedated!"* I laughed as I moved over to the coffee aisle and thought to myself, "I love my generation!" Many of us have memories of the old *Muzak* – popular music basically pushed through a grinder and stripped of all its soul, with words and guitars and drums all replaced by bland synthetic strings, a lead flute or soprano sax, and maybe a hint of drum machine. This music was then considered suitable for popular consumption in elevators, supermarkets, dentists' chairs, and other places desiring vanilla ambiance.

But not anymore. The Gen-Xers became the bosses and The Ramones became the elevator music. My consideration of this went beyond just chuckling among the Grape Nuts, however. I had to think, maybe this isn't very rock and roll. Punk rock in a supermarket? And not just supermarkets; this is the case with other areas of public life – TV commercials, shopping malls, doctors' and dentists' offices, and even children's music – all have started to rock. Is this allowed? Is it cool? Certainly there's the question of selling out. But I'm about bigger things: Is this still rock and roll?

God is a Rock God. Not a rock god like Little Richard and Mick Jagger and Janis Joplin and Eric Clapton and Robert Plant and Johnny Cash and David Bowie and Patti Smith and Bruce Springsteen and Stevie Nicks and Freddie Mercury and

Anne Wilson and Prince and Bono and Eddie Vedder and [insert your rock gods here]. God is a big-"G" God who reveals himself and his kingdom in rock and roll. But what does this mean?

At the beginning of this book, I wrote about Jimi Hendrix sacrificing his guitar at the 1967 Monterey Pop Festival. Two years before, there was another music festival that involved another fateful guitar performance. The Newport Folk Festival had hosted Bob Dylan in 1963 and 1964, where he was an up-and-coming golden boy lifting high the folk torch for the new generation. But when he took the stage in 1965, it was no longer just Bob and an acoustic guitar and harmonica. The unthinkable happened: Bob Dylan went electric. Playing a Fender Stratocaster and backed by an electric band, Bob launched into "Maggie's Farm" and then "Like a Rolling Stone" to a mixture of cheers and boos. This new sound characterized Dylan's new album and subsequent tour, which was met with the mixed reaction throughout, including the concert in Manchester, England, during which a fan yelled, "Judas!" (In response, Dylan called the man a liar and then told his band to play it loud!)

So what was the big deal? Why did an electrified Bob Dylan so bother not only the fans, but many of Bob's own heroes in the folk music community? The accusation was basically that Dylan had turned his back on his roots to become a rock star. Folk music is music of the people. It's music for singing along, for rallying others, for giving voice to the worker and the young and the oppressed and the voiceless. It isn't about volume and spectacle and rock star trappings. Bob Dylan couldn't be both a folkie and a rocker. Or could he?

What if, by going electric, Dylan was actually enlarging the music of the people? Perhaps he didn't like being pigeonholed, nor did he like "the people" being pigeonholed with one style of music. With hindsight it's clear that Bob Dylan had many stories to tell – stories of the people. And he found rock to be a suitable voice. Rock and roll is also roots music, the music of the people. Rock and roll was not born onstage. It was born in the fields and in the church. It's music for garages and front porches and street corners. Yes it blows the walls off of coliseums. But it always comes back to the street...to the people. This is the cycle of rock and roll.

There were the dark days of 1959, the end of the decade in which rock and roll music was born. At the beginning of the year, in February, pioneering rock genius Buddy Holly died in a plane crash with Richie Valens and The Big Bopper. Elvis was already in the Army. Little Richard had left rock and roll to become an evangelist. Jerry Lee Lewis had been blacklisted after marrying his 13-year-old cousin. And, closing out the year and the decade, in December, Chuck Berry got arrested. Not surprisingly, the "rock" music of the next few years was largely silly novelty songs and bland teen idols. Rock and roll itself might have lived fast and died young. But then the British Invasion came and brought back the rhythm and blues and love for the previous decade's originators that had been the soul of rock and roll. The Beatles, the Stones, and their mates reminded us of all that was good and pure about rock and roll music.

And so it has gone. The eventual mega-stardom and corporate copycat-ism of these same bands in the 60s gave rise to the simplicity of singer-songwriters in the 70s. As these singer-songwriters became homogeneous and rock became lite AM pop and oversized glam, punk came out of the garage and blew it all up. As raw funk turned into overproduced disco, New Wave streamlined it and heavy metal spit in its face. As "video killed the radio star" with the sea change brought by MTV, rap and hip-hop emerged wearing Adidas and shouting poetry from the streets, alternative rock jangled underground and shrugged at the superficiality of it all, and unruly thrash metal gnashed its teeth at camera-ready kings and queens of pop. Then the confetti good times of glam metal gave way to the raw turmoil of grunge. Corporately concocted boy bands and pop princesses were knocked from the charts by new singer-songwriters. Among overhyped hip-hop and slick dance pop came a new folk movement and a bluegrass revival. And the advent of independent production and internet broadcasting blew open both the demand and the supply for all manner of grassroots musical expression. And so the rock and roll cycle runs: things get big and slick and corporatized, and then the people step up with something simple and raw and authentic...something more rock and roll.

And so it is with the Rock God. Space doesn't permit tracing the similar pattern in the church. But suffice it to say, the cycle of birth, growth, soulless institutionalization, and grassroots revival throughout the history of Christianity would dwarf the paltry decades of rock and roll's pop culture struggles. The point is, God is a God of the people. He's not a product of the people, but a God who does not restrict his revelations or residency to an elite class or halls of power. Instead, he is Immanuel, literally "God with us." This is how he is revealed at the beginning of Matthew's Gospel with the fulfillment of Isaiah's prophecy, "'The virgin will conceive and give birth to a son, and they will call him Immanuel' (which means 'God with us')" (Matt. 1:23; Is. 7:14). And Jesus reminds his followers of the same thing at the end of Matthew's Gospel, "And surely I am with you always, to the very end of the age" (28:20). And these declarations bookend story after story of the good news that God has come in flesh to live and die and rise and make all things new, right in our midst.

This, indeed, is the entire story of Scripture. It's a story of the God who chooses to live and work inside his creation. Of course he's not bound by it, but he graciously chooses to reveal himself from within. And just as it begins with God working with the stuff of creation as a sculptor with clay (Gen. 2), and continues with very tangible revelations to and through the patriarchs and matriarchs and Moses and the prophets and Jesus and Paul and the church, so it all ends in the remade earth and heavens with the assurance from nothing less than God's own throne, "Look! God's dwelling place is now among the people, and he will dwell with them. They will be his people, and God himself will be with them and be their God" (Rev. 21:3).

Back on the coffee aisle, now with R.E.M.'s "Man On the Moon" playing. God is there, in shopping and drinking coffee, in going to work and coming home to family, in classrooms and boardrooms and living rooms and bedrooms, in arguments and stillbirths, in birthdays and funerals, in going to church and searching for meaning, in saying hello and saying goodbye. "Here's a truck stop instead of St. Peter's... yeah, yeah, yeah, yeah."[13] God is there. God is here, with us, rooted inside us. He is the Rock God, the God of fields and churches, of garages and front porches and street corners. The God of the people.

And so, yes, I think it's perfectly appropriate for The Ramones to play in supermarkets, for Aerosmith and Aretha to play while I try on shoes, for The Beach Boys and The Beastie Boys to play while I get my teeth cleaned, for The Cars and The Clash to play while I wait interminably for my doctor's appointment, for The Doors and The Dead to play while I eat a hamburger, for Elvis Presley and Elvis Costello to be elevator music. Rock and roll is music of the people, by the people, and for the people, and should be among the people. We don't save rock and roll for times when we jump on a Harley, light up a smoke, and leave our hometown behind. Rock and roll is all about our hometown. We move into the music. It's part of us, and we're part of it.

And this is the way of the Rock God, in whom "we live and move and have our being" (Acts 17:28). He isn't some distant deity we only encounter in a church building or in a "religious experience" or in death. We find him rooted in us, and we find ourselves rooted in him. He comes to us, and we leave ourselves behind to go to him. We leave the flash and bombast and rock star trappings and sold-out soullessness to return to the raw, the real, the Rock God who meets us in the cereal aisle.

TWENTY-ONE

REDEMPTION

THE FIRST SONG I LEARNED to play on guitar was Mötley Crüe's "Shout At the Devil." My brother had taught me some basic chords on the electric guitar I had and, with that illustrious beginning, I spent a lot of time in my bedroom learning the greats of 80s hard rock: the Crüe, Ratt, Dokken, Night Ranger, Bon Jovi, Van Halen, and the rest. One fateful day I went to the record store to get a new tape. I perused the tapes the way other boys looked at baseball cards – have it, have it, need it, have it, need it....For a reason unknown to me then, I ended up buying a tape by a band I'd never heard of. I didn't have a lot of money and never took chances with my hard-earned dollars (ok, I got my money from my mom, but still...). I went home and put this strange tape in the stereo and had my mind blown. The guitars wailed, the drums thundered, the singer screamed, all as well or better than the other bands I listened to. But the words were different.

Yes, you've busted me – it was Christian rock and the band was called Stryper. Under the band's name was a Bible reference: Isaiah 53:5. No other band had ever made me go look in a Bible, yet there it was: "But he was pierced for our transgressions, he was crushed for our iniquities; the punishment that brought us peace was upon him, and by his stripes we are healed." Deep stuff. The lyrics were in your face like the others I listened to. But instead of singing about abusing ourselves and desperate living and bloodstains on the stage, they sang about holding God's two-edged sword and standing up for what's right and light in the darkness. The childhood beliefs I very loosely held, the family tradition that sort of meant something to me but was mostly about being uncomfortable at Christmas and Easter, all of it came into laser focus and somehow became part of my teenaged rebellion. With a personality type and upbringing that was geared toward causes and activism, I now had a deeply personal cause that seemed to be of eternal significance. Then and there it began to shape my life, and it has ever since.

My best friends and garage bandmates joined me. We continued down the path of ripped clothes and long hair and piercings; we still rocked out to the old music. But we began studying Scripture and praying together and writing songs in keeping with our new direction. Other friends gave us a hard time about our musical choices. They just couldn't understand how people singing about God could sound so much like people singing about...well, less godly things. Much of it – the hair, the spandex, even some of the lyrics – seems silly now. But it was God speaking to me in a language I could understand: rock and roll. He reached me right where I was, in a record store. It seemed like a natural progression for me. But many of my fellow rockers laughed it off. Rock and roll is about rebellion, anti-establishment, good times. Christianity is about conformity, the institution, the humorless holiness of the frozen chosen. Right?

Rock and roll was born out of contradictions. It's the music of the Saturday night juke joint combined with the music of Sunday morning church – not one or the other. It's the high of rhythm and the low of blues. It's a raucous country stomp and an electrified city shuffle. It's simultaneously the music of slavery and the music of liberation. Rock and roll is about sin *and* redemption. We often miss that second part, but it's there. For every song about lost love there's a song about finding love. For every song about crying there's a song about dancing. For every song about being in prison there's a song about being free. For every song about loneliness and waywardness there's a song about friends and family and coming home. For every song about sex and drugs there's a song about...well, ok, maybe it comes up a little short.

But, as musician and producer and roots-music expert T-Bone Burnett explains it, "I learned early on that if you believe Jesus is the Light of the World there are two kinds of songs you can write – you can write songs about the Light, or about what you see by the Light."[14] How Christians approach the arts – or most other vocations and areas of life – is not a single, narrow path. And, truth be told, wouldn't we rather hear someone who is lost sing honestly about their lostness than a Christian sing falsely about being found and never having any more problems? Wouldn't we rather hear from someone vulnerably looking for answers than from someone acting like they have it all figured out? And then, of course, there are Christians telling authentic stories and there are plenty of non-Christians settled in to apathy, debauchery, and lies. There is hypocrisy and authenticity on both sides, to be sure. But labeling something Christian or not doesn't cut it, because Jesus never signed a record contract. The world we live in is a world of contradictions and tensions. This is as true for Christians as for anyone. We have our roots in the same soil as everyone else.

God's kingdom is juke joints and church, rhythm and blues, country and city, slavery and liberation, sin and redemption. This isn't to say that God's kingdom is a place of slavery and sin. But it is emerging among slavery and sin, within slaves and sinners. And despite our liberation, despite our redemption, we still fight to live free – at war with ourselves, with the world or the devil, with God knows what. We have been bought with blood, redeemed from slavery to sin and death and set free to live in eternal kingdom freedom...here and now! But, if we deny the tension and contradictions, we are armchair warriors defending cheap grace. We are living sleepily behind a holy façade that hides weak, ineffectual faith that has a form of godliness but lacks power. No, we live this faith with fellow strugglers, people getting it wrong on a daily basis, folk with polished shoes and pressed pants and bloodstained hands. But there're also saints with blemished faces and spotless souls, hard lives and soft hearts, scarred thoughts and sanctified minds. And we live in a world that continues to enslave, a world that is itself captive. All of it waits and trembles like a woman in the desperate pain of childbirth, waiting for the children of God to be revealed. If this isn't tension, I don't know what is.

And so, like rock and roll, we are rooted in redemption. Redemption is rooted in the cross. And the cross is very much rooted in this world. This kingdom of Christ's struggle and triumph, of *our* struggle and triumph, is sought and found in the same place where Eve took the fruit and Noah got drunk and Moses murdered the Egyptian and David committed deadly adultery and Herod slaughtered the innocents and Judas kissed Jesus and Paul stood by and watched Stephen get stoned to death – where the weeds grow right alongside the wheat. This is not an affront to God's plan. This *is* God's plan. The redemption story is not about you and me. It isn't even just about the church, at least not as we usually think of it. The redemption story is about the whole world. Just as the Rock God is a God of the people, working from within creation to bring it to fruition, so his Rock children are redeemed in order to do the same work. In Christ the work is done, but there's so much more to do. The world is saved, yet still so fallen. This is the tension. "Peace be with you! As the Father has sent me, I am sending you" (John 20:21). These are the words of the risen Christ to his cowering followers. There he stood, redemption finished but liberation just beginning.

This is the yell. It's the cry of the kingdom. It's the sound of deep silence and the wop-bop-a-loo-bop, a-lop bam boom! of ecstatic joy. The yell is inside us, yes. But, in the end, we find that we become part of the yell, echoing across the world and reverberating from life to life. We are singers of a song, picked up and passed on from one generation to the next. With a few riffs under our fingers and a new rhythm in our step, we rebel against what lies behind and we take to the road to play the music of the new world, a world rooted in eternity. We are newly born to sing a new song and to dance the dance of the Father and the Son and the Holy Spirit. We are remade to rock with the Rock God. Lace up your Chucks, plug in, and I'll count us off:

One, two, three, four…!

NOTES

Epigraphs:

Part I: David Bowie, quoted in Gordon Burn, "Bowie Holds Court," in the *Sunday Times Magazine*, November 30, 1980, http://www.bowiegoldenyears.com/articles/801130-sundaytimes.html.

Part II: Keith Richards, quoted in NPR Staff, "Keith Richards: 'These Riffs Were Built to Last a Lifetime'," November 13, 2012, http://www.npr.org/2012/11/13/165033885/keith-richards-these-riffs-were-built-to-last-a-lifetime.

Part III: Chuck Berry, "Rock and Roll Music," *One Dozen Berrys* (Chess, 1957).

Part IV: Jerry Garcia, Bob Weir, Phil Lesh, and Robert Hunter, "Truckin'," *American Beauty* (Warner Bros., 1970).

Part V: Bill Flanagan, *Written in My Soul: Conversations With Rock's Great Songwriters* (New York: Contemporary Books, 1986), ebook, Loc. 799.

[1] Angus Young, Malcolm Young, and Brian Johnson, "For Those About to Rock (We Salute You)," *For Those About to Rock (We Salute You)* (Albert Productions, 1981).

[2] From an MTV interview, the title or date of which I do not remember. I believe Lemmy was talking about the debates over censorship and a proposed record ratings system and, specifically, about the Parent's Music Resource Center (PMRC) of the 1980s.

[3] A fine example would be N.T. Wright's *Justification: God's Plan and Paul's Vision* (Downers Grove, IL: InterVarsity Press Academic, 2009).

[4] John Keats, "Ode on a Grecian Urn" (Public Domain).

[5] Wallace Stevens, "Anecdote of the Jar" (Public Domain).

[6] The image of an unfinished symphony to describe the currently incomplete state of earthly beauty owes to N.T. Wright's *Simply Christian: Why Christianity Makes Sense* (San Francisco: Harper Collins, 2006), pp. 39ff.

[7] This idea was most famously developed by John Duns Scotus (c. 1266-1308), especially in his *Ordinatio*. For an introduction to Scotus' thought, see Mary Beth Ingham's *Scotus for Dunces: An Introduction to the Subtle Doctor* (New York: Franciscan Institute Publishers, 2003).

[8] Flanagan, *Written*, Loc. 2697.

[9] *The Last Temptation of Christ*, directed by Martin Scorsese (Universal, 1988; Criterion, 2000), DVD.

[10] *Seinfeld*, "The Burning," Season 9 Episode 16, directed by Andy Ackerman (March 19, 1998; Sony Pictures Home Entertainment, 2007), DVD.

[11] Eugene Peterson, *A Long Obedience in the Same Direction: Discipleship In an Instant Society*, 2nd ed. (Downers Grove, IL: InterVarsity Press, 2000), p. 17.

[12] Eugene Peterson, *The Message: The Bible in Contemporary Language* (Colorado Springs: NavPress, 2002), pp. 2126-2127.

[13] Michael Stipe, "Man On the Moon," *Automatic For the People* (Warner Bros., 1992).

[14] Flanagan, *Written*, Loc. 6131.

ABOUT THE AUTHOR

Robert Pelfrey is a pastor, writer, and musician. He is an ordained Elder in Full Connection in the United Methodist Church, and a member of the New Mexico and Northwest Texas Annual Conferences of the United Methodist Church.

He studied music at Berklee College of Music in Boston and West Texas A&M University, theology at Regent College in Canada and Asbury Theological Seminary in Kentucky, and did doctoral work at the University of Manchester, England.

Robert has worked at churches of varying denominational identities, including Anglican, Baptist, Church of Christ, Methodist, and non-denominational charismatic and Bible churches.

He writes, teaches, and speaks in the areas of Spiritual Theology and Christian Formation. He blogs at www.RobertPelfrey.com and www.SalvationLife.com, and you can connect with him via Twitter @RobertPelfrey or at his website.

Robert and his family live in El Paso, Texas.

www.ingramcontent.com/pod-product-compliance
Lightning Source LLC
Chambersburg PA
CBHW051649040426
42446CB00009B/1056